Spiritual Truth in the
Age of Fake News

OTHER BOOKS BY ELIZABETH GEITZ

WWW.ELIZABETHGEITZ.COM

I Am That Child

Soul Satisfaction

Gender and the Nicene Creed

Calling Clergy

Fireweed Evangelism

Entertaining Angels

Spiritual Truth in the Age of Fake News

ELIZABETH GEITZ

RESOURCE *Publications* · Eugene, Oregon

SPIRITUAL TRUTH IN THE AGE OF FAKE NEWS

The Scripture quotations contained herein are from the New Revised Standard Version Bible, copyright 1989, by the Division of Christian Education of the National Council of the Churches of Christ in the U.S.A., unless otherwise noted. All rights reserved.

Because of the dynamic nature of the Internet, Web addresses or links may have changed since publication and may no longer be valid.

Reflections on pages 13-14, 59-60, 78-79, 94-95, 102-103, and 152-153 first appeared in the author's "Spirituality Matters" column in the Pike County Dispatch in Milford, Pennsylvania, and are used with permission of the editor.

In some instances, people's names have been changed to protect their identity.

Resource Publications
An Imprint of Wipf and Stock Publishers
199 W. 8th Ave., Suite 3
Eugene, OR 97401

www.wipfandstock.com

PAPERBACK ISBN: 978-1-7252-5294-3
HARDCOVER ISBN: 978-1-7252-5295-0
EBOOK ISBN: 978-1-7252-5296-7

Manufactured in the U.S.A.   12/10/19

To All Who Seek to Dwell in the Truth

"And Pilate asked Jesus, "What is truth?"
—JOHN 18:38

Contents

List of Illustrations   ix

Acknowledgments   xi

Preface   xiii

Reader's Guide   xvii

Feminine Imagery   1

Sexism   29

Racism   45

Heterosexism   65

Anti-Semitism   77

Xenophobia   87

Women Leaders   105

Survival   143

Epilogue   169

About the Author   173

Bibliography   175

Scripture Index   183

List of Illustrations

1. Elizabeth Geitz, "Hen Protecting Her Chicks." 2010, photograph of altar mosaic in Dominus Flevit Church, Mount of Olives, Jerusalem. 8"x10." Geitz Collection.

2. "Christ as a mother giving birth to the Church on the cross," detail from a *French Moralized Bible,* circa 1240, Bodleian Library, Oxford, England.

3. Suzanne Schleck, "Mary Magdalene Announcing the Resurrection to the Disciples," 2002, egg tempera and gold leaf on gessoed board, 11"x14," Pennsylvania, Geitz Collection. Original in the Albani Psalter, ca. 1123. Herzog August Biliothek, Wolfenbüttel.

Acknowledgments

I stand on the shoulders of countless women—from biblical women of faith and courage who risked it all to transcend the expected norms of their day; to Elizabeth Cady Stanton, who with twenty-six other women published *The Woman's Bible* in 1895; to the mentors in my personal life —my mother, Dorothy Bradley Rankin; Dr. Thayer Beach; the Rev. Dr. Margaret Guenther; Sister Lorette Piper; Sister Jane Mankaa; Annie Harris; and more.

I am truly grateful to Susan Keller and Dr. Kristen Murtaugh, my insightful editors; to Michael Elf, Esq., publishing advisor; and to Amy Ferris and Suzanne Braun Levine, who consistently encouraged me to write a book that sets the record straight on what the Bible says and does not say regarding key issues at this pivotal time in our nation's history.

Thank you from the bottom of my heart to those who read the manuscript and offered invaluable suggestions—Beth Cole, Joseph Fonlon, Esq., Suzanne Braun Levine, the Rev. James Harlan, the Rt. Rev. John Pritchard, the Rev. Burl Salmon, Sean Strub, Bruce Thall, Esq., Rev. Dr. Darla Dee Turlington, and Canon Constance White. Without each one of you, this book would be far less than it is.

Last, but never least, I thank my children, Charlotte and Mike, who have been here with me each step of the way—from my first book published in 1993 to this, my seventh book. What would I ever do without you? I am so proud to be your mother.

To the women who read my first book of biblical reflections, *Soul Satisfaction,* and shared your profound connection with the material, here's to you. Your stories have renewed my belief in the power of the written word to heal, to empower, and to teach. It was your pure joy of at last finding within the words of Scripture the abundant life God meant for you that urged me to write this more inclusive book dealing with the many different "isms" that still plague our world today.

Preface

Every morning the same words scream out of my newsfeed and bleed onto the screen. "Fake News! That's Fake News!" In a few short years, the phrase "Fake News" has earned a place in widely read dictionaries, educational games have been created about it, and legitimate news articles have been written about it.

But Fake News is not new. Fake News began when people first interpreted the Bible to advance their own agenda, and much of that interpretation was not questioned until women were allowed to study in seminaries and rabbinical schools.

Walk into any church, synagogue, or mosque and, regardless of theological differences, you will hear one consistent theme. God is depicted and spoken of almost exclusively as male. Yet in Scripture, God is described as a woman in labor giving birth to creation (Isaiah), a mother bear protecting her cubs (Hosea), a woman searching for a lost coin (Luke), and more.

What is the best way to counter Fake News? With the truth. To do so, I have turned to the Bible, the #1 best-selling book of the year every single year.[1] Whether you view yourself as religious or spiritual or neither, the world we all live in has been shaped by a

---

1. The words "Scripture" and "Bible" contained herein refer to the New Revised Standard Version of the Christian Bible composed of the Old and New Testaments. Completed in 1989, this translation is one of the most accurate. The Old Testament in Christian Bibles is primarily based on the Hebrew Bible or Jewish Tanakh.

patriarchal biblical worldview, a worldview based on the false belief that some people are second-class citizens and the Bible says it is so.

To ground us in our topsy-turvy world, I have countered this ultimate Fake News with the truth of what Scripture actually says. While I bring a Christian voice to the discussion, these reflections are not meant for Christians alone. It is hoped that people of different faiths or no faith will relate to the truth they convey.

Today many "isms" are experiencing resurgence—not only sexism but racism, heterosexism, anti-Semitism and more. Instead of moving forward, FBI statistics demonstrate that America is moving backward. The year 2017 saw an almost seventeen percent increase in hate crimes reported to the F.B.I. compared with the previous year.[2] What was unthinkable a few years ago is now seared into our minds with a parade of white supremacists in Charlottesville, Virginia shouting anti-Semitic slogans.[3] In a recent six-week period, there were attacks at a synagogue, churches, and mosques resulting in countless deaths.[4] Unarmed African American men like Botham Jean are shot and killed in their own apartment for no reason.[5] Hispanics were deliberately targeted in a Walmart massacre in El Paso, Texas in 2019.[6] Female candidates for President of the United States receive tougher coverage and less media exposure than their male counterparts,[7] and in 2016 LGBT Americans were "more than twice as likely to be the target of a violent hate-crime than Muslims or African-Americans."[8]

It's as if the progress made toward equality has been turned upside down. In this environment, *Spiritual Truth in the Age of Fake News* is needed more than ever. It is time to set the record straight on what the Bible actually says regarding the many "isms" alive and well today. It is time for the Fake News about the Bible to come to a

2. "2017 Hate Crime Statistics," para. 1.
3. Green, "Why the Charlottesville Marchers," para. 2.
4. Andone, "In the past 6 weeks," para. 1.
5. French, "The Worst Police Shooting," para. 2.
6. D'Anna, "This Anglo Came Here," para. 5.
7. Zremski, "Study: Women Presidential Candidates," para. 2.
8. Ifill, "LGBT Americans target," para. 1.

screeching halt. It is time for us to claim our inheritance of spiritual truth for all people.

We need to shout from the rooftops that there has never been a divinely ordained hierarchy that puts men above women, whites above other races, Christianity above other religions, straights above gays, or rich above poor. These are human constructs that have long outlived their time and that are against the very words of Scripture. Yes, this is the ultimate Fake News. Now more than ever, let us educate ourselves and allow these ancient words in their original meaning to nurture our very being.

I don't know about you, but I need to dwell in the truth. I need to proclaim that the Bible has been misused to support the very "isms" that are literally killing us.

Join me on this journey and, as you do, I pray that the spiritual truth our Creator wants for you will be yours. I pray you will find and be found by our Divine Mother, who loves you with an abundant and steadfast love, who never stops searching for you, no matter what.

Let her catch you. Come on! Turn the page.

Elizabeth Geitz
October 2019

Reader's Guide

To read straight through or to savor slowly? To use for personal reflection or in a group? To share what you discover within these pages or not to share? What is the best way to use the book you now hold in your hands?

The answer depends on your needs. *Spiritual Truth in the Age of Fake News* is adaptable to a variety of settings—individually for reflection or to help process the daily news; in a book group; in a religious group; and more.

I love to read something inspirational or thought provoking with my morning coffee, so savoring one reflection at a time fits the bill. If this works for you, you might try the following:

- Sit in a special chair or spot.

- Slowly read the passage of Scripture at the top of each page. Read it in the context of the NRSV translation. If you don't have a Bible handy, see https://bible.oremus.org.

- Read the passage again. What phrase jumps out at you? What is our Creator saying to you through this passage? Spend some time listening. As you do, what flows through your heart and mind?

- Now read the reflection. Meditate on the closing question. If you would like, journal about it.

- Sit with your thoughts and feelings. Ask yourself if you're called to action based on what you've read and experienced.

- If you wish to explore the topic further, go to the footnote sources.

- If you feel called to do so, share the True News with others.

If you prefer to focus on one topic, such as sexism, racism, or heterosexism, read the full chapter. Are you surprised at what you are reading in Scripture? What does your prior opinion of Scripture say about the world in which we live? What is your reaction to the many feminine images of God, the strong biblical women leaders, the biblical teaching on the many "isms" plaguing our world today?

If you're not someone who likes to spend time in reflection but find yourself overwhelmed by deliberately misleading news reports when you read or hear something—stop. If it relates to a topic in *Spiritual Truth in the Age of Fake News*, go to that chapter. Read what the Bible has to say about the subject when accurately translated. Don't simply accept what members of a religious group want you to believe. Study it for yourself by reading several reflections. If you feel called to do so, post part of the reflection on social media. (You have my permission. Just include a link to the book title and author's name.) *Counter Fake News with True News whenever possible!*

If you're in a book group, have members read the book in its entirety. Your discussion might focus on these questions:

- What most surprised you? Ask each person and listen. Move to the next person without discussion.

- Choose the chapter most often referenced. Have someone read a reflection from it aloud. Discuss. Read two more reflections from the same chapter. Discuss the closing questions.

- If time permits, choose a second chapter and do the same.

- OR ask each person in your book club to choose a reflection in advance that they would like to read aloud and discuss.

- At the end of your gathering, ask each person if they feel called to action in any of the areas discussed.

- Discuss how you might share this True News with others.

For Christian groups, *Spiritual Truth in the Age of Fake News* provides engaging material for Lenten and Advent Study Groups.

- Choose one chapter for each session. Ask participants to read the chapter in advance.
- Begin by agreeing on Group Norms. Suggested norms are:
    1. Listen to each other without interrupting.
    2. Give everyone a chance to speak.
    3. Speak respectfully.
    4. Keep politics out of the discussion (unless your group agrees it's a good idea to include politics).
- Ask each person to state in one sentence their reaction to the chapter. Proceed to the next person without discussion.
- Read one reflection from the chapter aloud. Discuss it as a group.
- Ask each person to reflect on the question at the end with one other person in the group. Have each pair share with the group, if desired.
- Move to another reflection in the same chapter and follow the same procedure.

For Jewish groups, the eight days of Pesach or Passover provide an opportunity to reflect on the portions of *Spiritual Truth in the Age of Fake News* that relate to the exodus journey. For instance, a focus on the women who aided that journey, such as Moses' mother, Jochebed; his sister, Miriam; and Rahab would be appropriate, as well as a reading of the reflections that deal with the Lord answering the cries of the enslaved Israelites. At any time, Jewish groups might want to engage the chapter on Anti-Semitism for clarity about this destructive aspect of historical Christian biblical interpretation.

For faith leaders of all traditions, the index in the back can be useful for sermon preparation.

Enjoy your journey!

Feminine Imagery

"He [God] has chosen to present Himself with an emphasis on masculine qualities of fatherhood, protection, direction, strength, etc. Metaphors used to describe Him in the Bible include: King, Father, Judge, Husband, Master, and the God and Father of our Lord Jesus Christ."[1]

Billy Graham Evangelistic Association

1. BGEA Staff, "Why does the Bible?" para. 2.

Thus says God, the LORD . . . "I will cry out like a woman in labor,
I will gasp and pant."

ISAIAH 42:5, 14

"What is your image of God?" I often ask, when leading workshops. Inevitably, responses are the same. "An old white man with a beard, a king, a judge, a father, a shepherd," are the replies. "Anymore?" I ask. "I don't see God as a person, more as a spirit," some add. "I see God most often in nature," others chime in.

"What about the image of our Creator as a woman in labor? Have you ever heard of that?" I ask. Blank stares and giggles come my way. "It's right here in the Bible. It really is," I say, pointing to this passage from the book of Isaiah. Heads shake in wonder.

Images of God as the Divine Feminine were not as unusual almost 3,000 years ago as they are today. In addition to Isaiah and other biblical writers, medieval mystics were especially fond of feminine images of our Creator. In the fourteenth century, the Christian mystic Meister Eckhart wrote: "God lies like a woman on a maternity bed who has given birth to every good soul that has learned to let go and is initiated."[2]

To represent our Creator exclusively as male gives both men and women a distorted image of the Divine that perpetuates the Fake News that God is male. The resulting patriarchal worldview has fostered inequality between the sexes that continues to this day.

In her book, *God Is Not A Boy's Name*, Lyn Brakeman writes, "It is idolatry to worship an all-male deity we know has no gender."[3] It is past time for this idolatry and the Fake News it perpetuates to end.

What a powerful image of the Creator of heaven and earth we are given in this passage from Isaiah. How affirming to both women and men. How might this inform your image of yourself? How could it change male/female dynamics today?

2. Quint, *Meister Eckhart,* 560, quoted in Fox, *Meister Eckhart: Mystic-Warrior,* 57.

3. Brakeman, *God Is Not A Boy's Name,* loc. 82.

For thus says the LORD . . . "As a mother comforts her child, so I will comfort you . . . You shall see, and your heart shall rejoice."

ISAIAH 66:12–14

Have you ever longed for a mother's comforting presence in times of trouble or for a comforting hug that can bring contentment and a sense of well-being? For those of us who have lost our mothers, this longing can linger for many years and seem never to leave.

Throughout Scripture, God is described as a comforting mother, a nursing mother, even a woman in labor. How strange and new these images may seem to us, yet they were written nearly three thousand years ago. The belief that God is not portrayed as female in Scripture is Fake News as old as the Bible itself.

Does this mean God is female? Of course not, no more so than God is male. God is beyond gender. Our Creator is beyond the confines of human language. For this reason, there is something called apophatic theology, which conveys that whatever God is, God also is not.

How does it work? Like this. While God is portrayed as father in Scripture, theologically God is and is not father. While God is portrayed as mother in Scripture, God is and is not mother. Because there are more images of God as father in Scripture, few people realize how many images there are of God as mother. Female images have been in Scripture all along to remind us that women, too, are indeed created in the image of God.

The imagery used to describe God has profound societal effects. Sarah Bessey writes, "Many of the seminal social issues of our time—poverty, lack of education, human trafficking, war and torture, domestic abuse—can track their way to our theology of, or beliefs about women, which has its roots in what we believe about the nature, purposes, and character of God."[4] Bringing feminine images of God out of the darkness of obscurity and into the light can and will change not only us, but the world in which we live.

How do you long to be comforted? Your Divine Mother can comfort you now, and more, much more than you can even ask or imagine. What would it feel like to put yourself in the presence of our Divine Mother?

4. Bessey, *Jesus Feminist*, 169.

I the LORD speak the truth . . . "Listen to me, O house of Jacob . . . who have been borne by me from your birth, carried from the womb; even to your old age I am he, even when you turn gray I will carry you. I have made, and I will bear; I will carry and will save."

ISAIAH 45:19, 46:3–4

In America, names have been assigned to different generations—the Greatest Generation (1910–1924), the Silent Generation (1925–1945), Baby Boomers (1946–1964), Gen-Xers (1965–1979), Millennials (1980–1994), Gen-Z (1995–2012), and finally Gen Alpha (2013–2025). Sociologists and psychologists studied and ascribed labels to each generation, trying to codify the individuality within it.

There's a lesser-known generation known appropriately as the Sandwich Generation, those people in their 40s or 50s who have a parent aged sixty-five or older and are also raising a youngster or supporting a grown child. Surprisingly, forty-seven percent of adults fit this category. "In fact, one in seven of these adults are financially assisting both their parents and one or more children."[5]

The stresses in such situations are myriad. Often, with both parents working, it is difficult if not impossible to meet not only the financial demands placed upon them but also the competing emotional demands. Nerves are frayed, self-care goes out the window, and tempers rise.

How comforting it is to know that our Divine Mother fills every need that we or our loved ones have from "womb to tomb." Our Creator carries us from the womb and still carries us when we turn gray. Each step of the life cycle, God is with our loved ones and with us. When we feel stretched beyond our limits, it is helpful to remember that we are not alone.

Can you talk to your Creator about the struggles in your own life to care for others, regardless of your age or theirs? Is there someone you need to put in your Divine Mother's loving care today?

---

5. "The Sandwich Generation," para. 2.

Listen to me, O house of Jacob, all the remnant of the house of Israel, who have been borne by me from your birth, carried from the womb . . . I have made, and I will bear; I will carry and will save . . . For I am God and there is no other.

ISAIAH 46:3–4, 9

In this age of social media, when we are connected in more ways than ever, an increasing number of people feel an aching loneliness. What was created to connect us to actual friends has instead led to connections with viral Facebook friends or Twitter and Instagram followers we will most likely never meet. Studies have shown that such connections can add vitality and communion to our lives. However, if we are spending hours each day on social media, feelings of loneliness and inadequacy can worsen. It is indeed Fake News that social media can fill our longing for human relationships on a deep and lasting level.

According to a 2018 survey by Cigna Health Insurance of twenty thousand Americans, "Nearly half of Americans report sometimes or always feeling alone (forty-six percent) or left out (forty-seven percent)."[6] As people continue to replace face-to-face or voice-to-voice interaction with social media communication or texting, such feelings will likely increase.

What can we do when we feel the desire, or even need, to scroll our social media feed for prolonged periods of time? Perhaps we can make a mental "stop" and remind ourselves that when we do so, we are not alone. We may feel alone, or even lonely, but this is a false sense.

This passage from the book of Isaiah brings into vivid relief that, not only does God bring us to birth, but our Divine Mother carries us throughout our lives. There are no loads too heavy, no words too difficult for our Creator to hear. Yes, God is described carrying us from the womb. The belief that God can be described only as male, or that God is male, is Fake News of the worst sort.

What might change if, instead of sharing your joys and sorrows with social media "friends," you shared them with your Divine Mother? Imagine the transformation that could result! Could that be the connection you yearn for but that often seems just out of reach?

Can you share something with your Divine Mother today? She is right beside you. Waiting.

6. Cigna, "New Cigna Study," para. 3.

*Then Moses went up to God; the L*ORD *called to him from the mountain, saying . . . "You have seen what I did to the Egyptians, and how I bore you on eagles' wings and brought you to myself."*

EXODUS 19:3-4

Eagle watching is a major pastime along the Delaware River, where I live, with eagle-cams prevalent during the winter season. Placed seventy-five feet high in a tree, thousands of viewers watch the eaglets hatch, learn to eat, and begin to fly, borne on their mother's wings. This wonder of nature can now be live streamed on computer screens, surely one of the wonders of modern technology.

Even so, many people prefer to do their eagle watching live, not live streamed. It is not unusual for such enthusiasts to arrive at a designated spot and wait for hours without a sighting. Then, through binoculars, they suddenly see a mother eagle. My brother told me of one such occasion, when he observed that the mother eagle had seen him, so he moved away to give her space to tend to her young.

Feeling safe, the mother eagle then gracefully flew toward her hungry eaglets with food in her talons. Rather than bringing the food to them, she placed it in a nearby tree, forcing them out of the nest. As the first eaglet faltered, the mother eagle flew under it and lifted it, then dropped away again when the eaglet could fly on its own. Several times my brother held his breath fearing an eaglet would fall to the ground, but each time it was safely swooped up on its mother's wings.

Following the Exodus journey, God tells Moses that God carried the Israelites to safety on eagles' wings. This image of a mother eagle teaching her young to fly is heartwarming. What a comforting image of our Creator, who is there to lift us when we fall. This is the True News that can comfort us when we, too, are afraid of falling.

What might it feel like to be carried on the wings of your Divine Mother?

You were unmindful of the rock who bore you; you forgot the God who gave you birth.

DEUTERONOMY 32:18

On the windswept Isle of Iona, available only by ferry, lie the ruins of an early thirteenth-century nunnery. While it contains the most complete remains of a medieval nunnery in Scotland, this is not what is most memorable about this crumbling ancient structure.

Like many convents of its time, it provided refuge for illegitimate girls, unmarried daughters, widows, and estranged wives. The nuns who founded it and lived there were of the Augustinian order. Nonetheless, precious mirrors, hairbrushes, and even a tiara were found among its ruins.

There is an interesting and unusual rock carving of a female above one of the outside windows. Called a Sheela Na Gig, it depicts a naked woman with large breasts and a large vulva in a squatting position. Interpretations of this ancient figure are numerous, ranging from a quasi-erotic female figure, to a dark goddess of sacred power, to a symbol to ward off evil.

Early Christians often took pagan symbols like this one, including erotic ones, and reinterpreted them to tell the Christian story. The squatting position in which the female figure is depicted in this carving was used to give birth in ancient times. Christians believe that God came into the world when Mary gave birth to Jesus. And so, this depiction of the birth process is thought to be a symbol to ward off evil spirits through the power of Christ.

How powerful such images can be for both women and men today. Here in this simple rock carving depicting the birth of Jesus, we are reminded that the Divine Feminine not only birthed Jesus but birthed each one of us as well.

What does it mean to you that God gave you birth? What could it mean?

Then Job answered (God) . . . "Did you not pour me out like milk and curdle me like cheese? You clothed me with skin and flesh, and knit me together with bones and sinews. You have granted me life and steadfast love, and your care has preserved my spirit."

JOB 9:1, 10:10–12

In the bestselling novel, *The Shack*, God is portrayed as an African American woman named Papa. As the book opens, we meet Papa as a female homemaker filled with steadfast love for all, much like our Creator is portrayed in this passage from Job. The main character in the book, Mack, had a six-year-old daughter who was brutally murdered, and he is devastated. Four years later Papa summons him with a note to the shack where his daughter was killed, and Mack courageously goes.[7]

What awaits him there is a life-changing experience of the Divine as an African American female, of Jesus as a Middle Eastern male, of the Holy Spirit as an Asian female with a Hindu name, and, near the end of the book, of God as a Native American. Of the novel's Trinitarian portrayal of the Divine, Richard Rohr writes, "For the first time since fourth-century Cappadocia, the Trinity actually became an inspired subject of conversation and rather pleasant questioning in homes and restaurants. And it continues!"[8]

The power of these diverse images is overwhelming, both inside and outside the novel. With twenty-six million copies sold worldwide, the book has struck a chord deep within the soul of many. People long for an entry into the Divine, an ability to see themselves in the images used to describe our Creator, who is beyond the capacity of any one image to contain. Here women, men, blacks, Asians, Middle Easterners, and Native Americans can all see themselves portrayed in the Divine. How unlikely this book's popularity is, yet how refreshing and instructive it can be.

The prevailing view that God is portrayed only as father in Scripture, as perpetuated by the Billy Graham Evangelistic Association and others, is Fake News. The True News is that diverse images

---

7. Young, *The Shack*, 16.
8. Rohr, *The Divine Dance*, loc. 340.

of God abound in Scripture, adding to the richness of who our Creator is and who our Creator is not.

In churches, synagogues, and mosques today, diverse images of God are largely absent. Perhaps *The Shack* has something to teach us about imagery of the Divine. Perhaps, more importantly, the Bible has something to teach us.

Let those who have ears to hear, hear.

Then the LORD answered Job out of the whirlwind . . . "Who shut in the sea with doors when it burst out from the womb?"

JOB 38:1, 8

Recently there has been an increase in hurricanes battering the Eastern shores of the United States, packing winds of ninety miles per hour or more. Those in a hurricane's path are often forced to flee for their lives on traffic-choked highways, hoping they will escape the deadly winds and rising water.

Seas are angry, churned up, raging at something felt but not seen. Reminding me of the Lord's answer to Job out of the whirlwind, the seas appear to be bursting out from the very womb of our Divine Mother.

This powerful feminine image of the womb of God is a memorable one with waters bursting forth like the rush of water that precedes human birth. The process of the death and destruction nature can bring is as unpredictable as the process that brings forth new life, new birth.

But some things are indeed predictable. If we humans keep ignoring the disastrous effects of climate change, there will be a steady increase in the number of "torrential hurricanes, devastating droughts, crippling ice storms, and raging heat waves . . . that claim lives and cause untold damage."[9] Climate change deniers participate in well-orchestrated Fake News that goes against scientific studies the world over, Fake News that has led to the extinction of hundreds of animal and fish species.

God is weeping at our lack of care for the earth entrusted to our stewardship, at the selfish pride that keeps us believing that, in spite of scientific evidence to the contrary, we are not responsible for the devastation caused by our action and inaction.

The seas will continue to burst forth from God's womb in ways that can bring new life or new destruction. Which will it be? What could you do to make a difference?

9. National Geographic, "Five Ways Climate Change," para. 11.

It was you (God) who took me from the womb; you kept me safe on my mother's breast.

PSALM 22:9–10

It all began on a trip to Oberammergau, Germany, home of the 380-year tradition of Passion Plays. They are performed only in years ending in zero, and, unfortunately, I visited in an off year. But the city is also known for woodcarvings, and there are beautiful nativities in every store window. I bought one for a souvenir, and a collection was born. With great delight I now look for locally-made nativities whenever I travel, marveling at the different materials used—from straw, to gourds, to finely fired ceramic, to exotic woods.

After carefully assembling my collection last year, I began to wonder if perhaps someone was missing. So, I did some research. Could it be that the trusted midwife is left out of the familiar Christmas story and hence nativity sets?

Christine Schenk, a theologically trained nurse/midwife, has this to say. "In first-century Palestine, it would have been inconceivable for a woman to give birth without the care and comfort of other women . . . Even though Mary and Joseph were far from home, hospitality was pretty much the prime directive for the people of Palestine . . . So I'm guessing the innkeeper, or more probably his wife, saw Mary's plight and sent for the wise women of Bethlehem to come and tend to her."[10]

Could it be that Joseph knew how to deliver a baby? It is highly unlikely. As Schenk writes, the gospel of Luke was clearly written by a man who skipped over every detail of the birth process. "Of the actual birth we learn only the basics: It was time. The baby was born. We wrapped the baby in blankets. And that's pretty much it folks."[11]

The image of God as a midwife is a powerful metaphor. Throughout our lives, all of us need to be midwifed in various ways. We may not need assistance in the physical birth process, but we often need to be midwifed through one of life's many transitions. After the birth of a child, all parents need to be midwifed through the confusing process of parenting. When we change careers, we

10. Schenck, "There would have been a midwife," para. 11–12.
11. Schenck, "There would have been a midwife," para. 7.

need to be midwifed through the transition. When we retire, we need a different kind of midwife, one who can help us navigate the array of possibilities before us. And, in that final transition from life to death, we all need a trusty midwife by our side.

Is there an area of your life in which you need to let your Divine Mother be your midwife? Can you put yourself in God's hands and simply trust?

For you created my inmost being; you knit me together in my mother's womb.

PSALM 139:13

Could it be that God enjoys knitting on a rainy afternoon? Apparently so. Our Divine Mother never ceases to amaze me. I have just finished knitting a red and black sweater which was supposed to be completed by Christmas, then by Valentine's Day, then by my summer birthday. Finally, in September, after almost two years in the making, my sweater was finally finished.

I proudly wore it for the first time to rave reviews. Over many years of marriage, my husband has learned to compliment me endlessly on such endeavors. Nevertheless, even I must admit it looks pretty good. What fascinates me is that the sweater is full of mistakes, mistakes only I know are there. How much like our lives, my little sweater is!

The single black stitches within it are supposed to be evenly spaced, making symmetrical dots on the red background. Yet one is too high, another too low, another too large, another almost disappearing into the red . . . that is, if you know where to look.

Then there's the mega-mistake on the sleeves—black dot problems again. In order to bend your arm, the width of a sleeve must be increased at the elbow, yet the instructions said nothing about continuing with the black dots. Voila! An entire section of each sleeve is solid red with no black in sight. What to do? Just turn the sleeve around when you wear it, so no one notices.

And truth be told, there are times in our lives when we need to do the same. Not every mistake we've ever made needs to be shared with the world. With a trusted friend or spouse? Yes. The world? No. Keeping some things as close to our chest as those solid, mixed-up inner sleeves of mine is prudent.

Then there's the collar. Somehow, I ended up knitting it wrong side out. Not one person has noticed. Not one. It was supposed to stand up, but, no, it flops. The flopping is beyond my control. It simply flops. Some things, many things, in life are simply beyond our control. There is nothing we can do about it. What to do? Stop trying to control it. Just accept it and keep going.

Then there's the biggest fiasco of the entire sweater. When I finished, it was a perfect fit for a child. Seriously. All my friends laughed whenever they saw me working on it. "Is that a dog sweater?" "Is it for your four-year-old granddaughter?"

In desperation, I ran to the local knit shop. The owner calmly said, "No problem; we'll add gussets." So, I added gussets to each side. The sweater was way too small because my stitches were too tight. The learning? Relax! Being uptight doesn't help us or anyone around us or our sweater that can end up five sizes too small. Some of us must learn to relax and, yes, it's worth it.

And finally? Accessorize. The sweater went from buttons all the way down the front, to two buttons at the top, to maybe one button, to "let's put a frog on it and call it a day!" So, I went to the garment district in New York City and found the most glamorous crystal frog ever made. It dazzles. It's stunning. And, yes, it takes your eye away from the many mistakes.

We've all made them. We all have them. But no one is aware of them like we are. No one else even cares. They just see the final product and smile—for God knit us together in our mother's womb, and God does not make mistakes.

Thus says the LORD: "We have heard a cry of panic, of terror, and no peace. Ask now, and see, can a man bear a child? Why then do I see every man with his hands on his loins like a woman in labor? Why has every face turned pale?"

JEREMIAH 30:5–6

Is God depicted in the Bible as having a sense of humor? Absolutely! Just as we are told throughout Scripture that our Creator weeps with us, God also laughs with us. Consider this verse from Psalm 37, "The wicked plot against the righteous, and gnash their teeth at them, but the Lord laughs at the wicked for he sees that their day is coming." It can be difficult to imagine, but there it is. Similarly, Psalm 2 tells us that "He who sits in the heavens laughs" at earthly kings who take their stand against the Lord. This can be comforting to those who lament the evil done by earthly rulers today who seem to answer to no one. Make no mistake; they do.

Not only is our Creator depicted in Scripture as laughing, God can also tell a good joke. I can almost hear the laughter when the Lord teases the men that they look like women in labor, with their faces pale and their hands on their loins. How unlikely this comparison must have been almost 3,000 years ago. How unlikely it still is today, but here it is recorded for all time.

Deepak Chopra says, "the healthiest response to life is laughter."[12] Laughter is contagious, reduces the stress response, boosts immunity, increases resilience, combats depression, and more.[13]

If we can laugh at ourselves and at our situation, whatever it may be, our burdens will certainly be lighter. If we take life too seriously and never step back to put it in perspective, we can indeed lose our groundedness. The prevailing view that God is primarily a stern father and judge is more Fake News. Lest we forget that God has a sense of humor, perhaps we need to keep this passage close at hand. Our Creator can be a role model for us here.

12. Lechner, "6 Reasons Why Laughter," para. 4
13. Lechner, "6 Reasons Why Laughter," para. 6.

Also, when we forget that God does indeed have the proverbial last laugh, we can easily become depressed at events around us. Let us never forget who ultimately rules and who does not.

What might happen if you shared something humorous with your Divine Creator, right now? Come on. Try it!

*I have been the L*ORD *your God ever since the land of Egypt . . . I will fall upon them like a bear robbed of her cubs.*

HOSEA 13:4, 8

One sunny day my husband, children, and I were swimming in the pond on our farm in northeast Pennsylvania. When the children weren't pushing us off our rafts, Michael and I were lazily drifting in the water. Those family times remain some of my happiest memories. Yet one day stands out in vivid relief for a different reason. Suddenly, we all saw what appeared to be an alligator in the far end of the pond. We were frightened out of our wits.

We quickly hurried our children out of the pond, remembering the adage that most animals can move far faster than humans. Nonetheless, there seemed to be no alternative.

To our shock, we soon discovered that the "alligator" was a mother bear submerged in the water with just the tip of her back and nose showing. As we stood on the opposite bank in awe, a five-hundred-pound bear emerged and slowly sauntered over to her cubs who had been hiding in the woods nearby. She then guided them to safety, oblivious to all of us who had disturbed her quiet reverie in the cool water.

Mother bears have tremendous affection for their cubs, at times holding them close for comfort, at other times fighting for their protection or guiding them to safety. The image of God as a mother bear is one that speaks to me deeply. Yes, we have a Creator who comforts us, fights for us, and guides us to safety. I don't know about you, but I need a God who will fight for me tooth and nail if need be. Comfort is good, but sometimes more is needed to feel truly safe. Can you recall a time when you needed God to protect you, to fight for you against the enemy within or the enemy without? Can you remember a time when God did that for you?

What might happen if you called on Mother Bear?

(Jesus said), "Jerusalem, Jerusalem, the city that kills the prophets who are sent to it! How often have I desired to gather your children together as a hen gathers her brood under her wings, and you were not willing!"

LUKE 13:34

As pilgrims in the Holy Land, our group walked down the wet, slippery hill in beating rain that turned my umbrella inside out. Knees wet, feet slipping, heads bowed against the wind, we walked in single file. Below us lay the tear-shaped Church of Dominus Flevit, which means, "the Lord has wept." The weather set the mood for our visit to this place where Jesus overlooked the city of Jerusalem and wept for his people who could not recognize those things that meant peace.

Oceans of blood have been spilled in Jerusalem since that day when Jesus stood there and looked down at the city where he would soon be crucified. Jesus wept then and Jesus weeps now for the inability of people to come together as God's children, to see their commonalities rather than their differences.

On the front of the altar in this tiny church is the colorful mosaic of a powerful feminine image of Jesus, that of a mother hen who longs to gather her brood under her wing. Jesus did not shy away from describing himself with this maternal image to express the depth of his love for his people. He wept because they "were not willing" to come within his loving embrace.

The belief that Jesus never spoke of himself in feminine terms and that he cannot be so portrayed is nothing more than Fake News. Both Augustine and Anselm of Canterbury quoted Jesus' portrayal of himself as a mother hen. In the year 1093, Anselm wrote: "But you, Jesus, good Lord, are you not also a mother? Are you not that mother who, like a hen, collects her chickens under her wings? Truly, master, you are a mother."[14]

The priest who was guiding us on that rainy afternoon in Jerusalem solemnly looked at the colorful altar mosaic and said, "The feminine *is the answer* to the violence and lack of peace over which Jesus weeps."

14. Bynum, *Jesus as Mother*, 114.

How might our world be different if more leaders of nations were women?

"Hen Protecting Her Chicks," Modern altar mosaic in the Church of Dominus Flevit,
Mount of Olives, Jerusalem
Photo credit: Elizabeth Geitz, 2010

Or what woman having ten silver coins, if she loses one of them, does not light a lamp, sweep the house, and search carefully until she finds it? When she has found it, she calls together her friends and neighbors, saying, "Rejoice with me, for I have found the coin that I had lost."

LUKE 15:8–9

Have you ever searched tirelessly under furniture for that one, small, lost toy of a child? More than once, I have turned over every cushion in the house looking for one of my children's prized possessions whether it's a special toy, a tiny coin, or some other newfound gem.

I have also gotten down on my hands and knees to search for a lost cell phone. Who among us has not searched high and low for this "can't live without it" commodity of today's world? When it is lost, we rack our brains trying to remember where we last saw it, and we don't stop looking until we find it.

When the search is over, there is always a sigh of relief, great rejoicing and a sense of completeness. How comforting it is to know that our Creator searches for us with this same intensity until we are safely in the palm of our Divine Mother's hand.

A familiar image of God is that of a male shepherd searching for one lost sheep. However, the belief that this is the only image of God searching for one lost soul is, you guessed it, more Fake News. In the gospel of Luke, immediately after the passage of God searching for a lost sheep, lies a little-known treasure. Here, God is described as a woman who diligently sweeps her house in search of one lost coin. What a compelling image of the Divine Feminine! How true to life it is.

In the 1613 painting, *The Parable of the Lost Drachma*, Italian artist Domenici Fetti vividly portrays God as a woman turning over every chair and bench in her humble home to find that one lost coin.[15] The lost coin is a drachma, one of the basic silver coins of the Greeks.[16] "A third-century-BC source says the drachma was the price of a sheep or one-fifth the price of an ox."[17]

15. Fetti, *Parable of the Lost Drachma*, 1618.
16. DeBloois, "Coins in the New Testament," 241.
17. Arndt and Gingrich, cited in *A Greek-English Lexicon*, 242.

In 1836, French artist James Tissot beautifully captured this image of God in a watercolor painting. Portrayed as a woman in biblical dress, our Divine Mother is shown on her hands and knees peering under and sweeping under a large basket.[18]

Isn't it amazing that the Divine Feminine never ceases to search for us, regardless of how long we may be lost? Could she be searching for you?

18. Tissot, *The Lost Drachma*, 1886–1894.

*Jesus . . . said to them . . . "A little while, and you will no longer see me,
and again a little while, and you will see me . . . Very truly I tell you,
you will weep and mourn, but the world will rejoice; you will have
pain, but your pain will turn into joy. When a woman is in labor, she
has pain, because her hour has come. But when her child is born, she
no longer remembers the anguish because of the joy of having brought
a human being into the world. So you have pain now; but I will see
you again, and your hearts will rejoice."*

JOHN 16:16, 20–22

When Jesus shares the central event of his ministry with his disciples, that he will soon die but they will see him again, he can think of no better image to capture the pain and joy of that experience than a woman in labor giving birth. Men of his day rarely, if ever, discussed the birthing process, yet Jesus brings it into the light as the sacred experience it is.

Upholding the feminine as participating in the divine act of creation, Jesus once again teaches the sacredness of being female, this time by his words.

He also shares a deep truth that can be experienced by all of us, male or female, that our deepest pain can also be turned into the greatest joy. Twenty-eight years ago, when my mother took her own life, I experienced emotional pain unlike anything I had known existed. I cried out to Jesus to be with me, comfort me, give me hope for a better tomorrow. In those moments, I intensely felt his presence filling me with a peace that passes all understanding, a joy that has lasted far beyond that moment.

It is often said that those who have experienced the deepest sadness can experience the greatest joy, and I can attest to that truth in my own life. With faith in a power far greater than our own, our pain, too, will turn into joy.

Is there a life experience you need to put into the hands of your loving Creator?

From noon on, darkness came over the whole land until three in the afternoon . . . Then Jesus cried again with a loud voice and breathed his last.

MATTHEW 27:45, 50

Christians believe that the agony of Christ on the cross is the agony of the birth pangs of a new creation. Just as God gives birth to creation and endures the pains of labor on our behalf, so, too, does Jesus endure that pain when he gives birth to the new creation on the cross. Through the crucifixion, Jesus experiences something not unlike the desperate pain of a mother dying in childbirth.[19]

Christ giving birth to the Christian church on the cross is vividly depicted in a thirteenth-century French Bible illumination. In the image, the church is depicted as a baby being born out of Christ's side.[20] It startled me when I first discovered it. It seemed so odd. On the top portion of the cross, just above this image, is a depiction of Eve being born out of the side of Adam from his rib. This image was more familiar. Then I began to see the connection. Paul describes Jesus as the new Adam, ushering in a new creation. Both Adams, in a sense, give birth.

It is highly unusual today for anyone to talk about a man giving birth. Yet in Scripture, Jesus is described as giving birth to the church. When viewed alongside the passages of God as a mother and of Jesus describing himself as a mother, it is clear that centuries ago people were more comfortable with the feminine than they seem to be today. Sharing this True News with others can give birth to new understandings of what it means to be female and male.

How might our lives be different, if we could believe that Christ gave birth on the cross to new life?

19. Geitz, *Gender and the Nicene Creed*, 55.
20. Geitz, *Gender and the Nicene Creed*, 60.

"Christ as a mother giving birth to the Church on the cross,"
detail from a French Moralized Bible, *circa 1240.*
Bodleian Library, Oxford, England
Photo credit: Bodleian Library Imaging Services

Since, therefore, God's children share flesh and blood, he himself
likewise shared the same things . . . Therefore he had to become like
his brothers and sisters in every respect, so that he might be a merciful
and faithful high priest in the service of God.

HEBREWS 2:14, 17

How can women possibly be clergy, since Jesus, the faithful high priest, was male? This question has thwarted the call of countless women to ordained ministry throughout the centuries.

Fortunately, a sound theological understanding of the particular traits of the human Jesus, known as the "particularity of Jesus," changes the discussion. Jesus of Nazareth was a Middle Eastern Jewish male. Yet how many Gentile men have been told that they cannot be ordained because they are not Jewish? I would venture to say, none. But women throughout the ages have been told that another aspect of who Jesus is, his gender, bars them from serving in a clerical capacity.

Paul's Letter to the Hebrews makes it clear that as the Christ, or the Divine on earth, Jesus transcends gender distinctions. Christians believe that Jesus was both human and divine. Through his divinity, Jesus becomes "like his brothers and sisters in every respect." Therefore, women are not only made in the image of God but in the image of Jesus, as well. This is the True News!

In *Women at the Well*, Kathleen Fischer writes, "Women's imaginations need the deep emotional healing and affirmation that come from seeing the image and likeness of Christ conveyed more fully in relation to them . . . To say that Christ cannot be imaged as a woman is to imply that women cannot, in fact, image Christ."[21]

Realizing that Jesus became like his brothers and sisters in every respect is life-changing for women who felt excluded from portraying themselves in his likeness. This is the True News! What different message does this send to you? Is there someone with whom you are called to share it?

---

21. Fischer, *Women at the Well*, 81.

Paul an apostle . . . To the churches of Galatia . . . "My little
children, for whom I am again in the pain of childbirth until Christ
is formed in you."

GALATIANS 4:1, 19

These words of Paul are tender, gentle, and straight from the heart. His love for his children in the faith is so great that, when they don't understand what it means to follow Christ, he can think of no better way to describe the depth of his pain than that of the birth process. How many men today would describe their emotional pain in this way? Not many. Yet Paul does not shy away from using this powerful feminine imagery in relation to himself. The belief that Paul never used feminine images to describe himself is more Fake News that misrepresents Paul's understanding of himself and of women.

In this passage, Paul is also letting his followers know that he is willing to die for them. In the first century, it was not unusual for a woman to die during or soon after childbirth. When we envision the experience of childbirth in a hospital setting today, most of us can easily miss the richness and sense of sacrifice embodied in this passage. Our sisters in developing nations do not have the luxury of our birthing centers. For example, in Cameroon, West Africa, one in six women still die during childbirth, an abysmal, preventable reality.

According to a 2015 World Health Organization report, in the United States the maternal mortality rate between 1990 and 2013 "more than doubled from an estimated twelve to twenty-eight maternal deaths per 100,000 births."[22] A 2010 Amnesty International report states that maternal mortality in the U.S. is the highest when compared to forty-nine countries in the developing world, with "African-American women three to four times more likely to die from pregnancy-related causes than white women."[23] This appalling statistic brings us to the reality that childbirth results in death far too often today and that something must be done to change this deadly trend.

Paul's portrayal of himself as a woman in labor willing to die for what he believes can put us in touch with our sisters in America

22. Agrawal, "Maternal Mortality," para. 1.
23. Amnesty International, "The US Maternal Health Crisis," para. 3, 6.

as well as with our sisters in developing nations who lose their lives in this tragic and preventable way.

What one act could you undertake to help change these abysmal statistics?

Paul, Silvanus, and Timothy, To the church of the Thessalonians . . .
"We were gentle among you, like a nurse tenderly caring for her own
children . . . you have become very dear to us."

1 THESSALONIANS 1:1, 2:7–8

I'll never forget the night I missed seeing Luciano Pavarotti in concert. My husband and I had been given free tickets to hear one of the finest Italian opera singers of all times. Six weeks prior to the date, I had given birth to our first child. As a nursing mother, everything was new to me. I had yet to master the use of a breast pump and, to be honest, I was afraid I would, yes, leak on my dress. So, to avoid embarrassment I stayed home and watched the production on television while nursing our infant daughter.

Nursing an infant is sacrificial on many levels, not just when missing a world-renowned opera star! The mother must eat well, hydrate regularly, and attempt to stay rested despite being awakened several times a night by a crying baby. A nursing mother cannot leave her child for long until a regular schedule is maintained. Overwhelming love of a near-sacred dimension mingled with a sense of self-sacrifice are the conflicting feelings which many nursing mothers experience.

The Greek word Paul uses for "nurse" is *trophos,* which means "caregiver," a person who sustains someone else by nourishing and offering them the tender care of a nurse. It holds the "connotation of a mother's care, of holding a child close, wrapped in her arms."[24]

When Paul, Silvanus, and Timothy want to express the tenderness they feel for the people of Thessalonica they compare themselves to a nursing mother. What a powerful feminine image of selfless love and compassion. How unselfconsciously theses three men describe themselves in feminine terms.

What clues might this give us regarding Paul's view of women?

24. Trotter, "Why the Apostle Paul," para. 7.

Sexism

"Our biblically assigned role is to submit to the men God placed in authority over our lives."[1]

Dr. Rhonda H. Kelley
New Orleans Baptist Theological Seminary

"Feminism is doomed to failure because it is based on an attempt to repeal and restructure human nature."[2]

Phyllis Schlafly

1. Zauzmer, "What Draws Women," para. 15.
2. Lewis, "Phyllis Schlafly," para. 7.

*So God created humankind in his image, in the image of God
he created them, male and female he created them . . . God saw
everything that he had made and indeed, it was very good.*

GENESIS 1:27, 31

There are two different creation accounts in the book of Genesis. In the above account, male and female are created at the same time as equals. Neither is described as superior to the other.

The fullness, the beauty, the equality of male and female inherent in this passage have been ignored throughout history, perpetuating the Fake News that women are inferior to men. In this account, God created male and female simultaneously. Thus, women as well as men are created in the image of God and reflect that image in their lives. The casting aside of such passages has enabled skewed male/female dynamics to flourish.

Worldwide, thirty-four million female adolescents are not in school, and two-thirds of the illiterate people in the world are female.[3] Women the world over still perform the majority of cleaning, cooking, and child-rearing tasks, and, in the American workplace, there is a significant gender pay gap harmful to women's economic security. And the origin of such inequality? Fake News regarding the inferiority of women in sacred Scripture.

Regardless of how far women advance, the discrepancies still hold true. Today women hold only twenty-three percent of U.S. Congressional seats, while men hold seventy-seven percent; the United States has never had a female president or vice-president, and two out of three Supreme Court justices are male. In addition, a recent study by the Harvard Business Review shows that "male justices interrupt the female justices approximately three times as often as they interrupt each other during oral arguments."[4]

Such realities and the visual images they evoke communicate powerful messages to women and men throughout the world. Equally powerful is the use of only male images to describe God, even though such exclusive imaging is not in keeping with biblical tradition.

3. UNESCO, "Education for All," para. 2, 4.
4. Jacobi and Schweers, "Female Supreme Court," para. 1.

We are all created in God's image, and we are indeed very good. God has said so. How might you incorporate this belief into your everyday life?

And God said to them, ". . . have dominion over the fish of the sea and over the birds of the air and over every living thing that moves upon the earth."

GENESIS 1:28

Historically, the Bible has been used to justify the dominion of man over woman. Yet in the first creation account in Genesis, both male and female are created in the image of God; neither gender is given dominion over the other.

What God does do is give both woman and man dominion over every living thing that moves upon the earth. "It has been argued that human exploitation of the nonhuman world finds here its ungodly warrant. Moreover, starting in seventeenth-century England, this verse began to be read by some as endorsing total human control over all nature."[5] Unfortunately, this view has persisted until our own time.

But is this what dominion means in this passage? Far from it. The Hebrew word used for "dominion" does not mean "to dominate" or "to exploit." It means "to take responsibility for." What a difference this correct understanding makes! Humans are meant to be good stewards of creation, to care for the world which God created, to wisely manage the abundant resources Mother Earth has given to us.

"Therefore, being stewards of creation is foundational to what it means to be human. Caring for creation is not an add-on, not a sideline, not related just to part of our calling. It represents our proper human relationship to Earth. This portrayal puts human beings squarely in a caretaker position in regard to environmental stewardship."[6]

Yet people the world over have not heeded this call. A wide-ranging study released in May 2019 states, "Nature is declining globally at rates unprecedented in human history—and the rate of species extinction is accelerating . . . The Report finds that around one million animal and plant species are now threatened with

5. Davis, *Opening Israel's Scriptures,* loc. 379.

6. Rhoads, David, "The Stewardship of Creation: A Theological Reflection," *Lutherans Restoring Creation,* October 2018, para. 5.

extinction, many within decades, more than ever before in human history . . . More than forty percent of amphibian species are threatened."[7]

When I see tons of plastic waste strangling life in our oceans, I wonder how we humans could be so short-sighted. When I see one environmental regulation after another being rolled back, I know the answer. As long as Americans put corporate profits above a sustainable environment, we will continue down the dangerous trajectory on which we find ourselves. As long as Americans put their own perceived needs above the needs of Mother Earth, we will continue to pollute the life-sustaining creation God gave us, ultimately polluting ourselves.

We can no longer ignore human contributions to increased greenhouse gas emissions, which have doubled since 1980.[8] We can no longer ignore the global interconnectivity of all human activity. We can no longer ignore our own role in contributing to these abysmal statistics.

How can we best live into our call to be stewards of God's creation? What one action could you take to make a difference?

7. Intergovernmental Science-Policy Report, para. 1, 9.
8. Intergovernmental Science-Policy Report, para. 1, 9.

Then the Lord God said, "It is not good that the man should be alone;
I will make him a helper as his partner . . . And the rib that the Lord
God had taken from the man he made into a woman."

Genesis 2:18, 22

In this second, more familiar creation account in Genesis, the woman is created out of the rib of the man to be his helper. When words are translated into English, important shades of meaning can be lost.[9] The English word "helper" is often used to describe someone in the role of an assistant. However, this is not the meaning of the original Hebrew.

The Hebrew words translated as "helper," literally mean "a helper corresponding to" the one being helped. Before the creation of woman, the man has only animals with which to relate, whereas the focus here is on the unique way humans relate. The Hebrew words for "helper" are used sixteen times in Scripture to speak of God's direct assistance to human beings. A word used in reference to our Creator does not indicate secondary status.

Yet, over 5,000 years after these words were written, women are still not treated equally, in large part due to the weaponization of Scripture. This abuse of the Bible is persistent Fake News. The recent #MeToo Movement has brought into graphic relief the unequal treatment and sexual harassment of women in almost every profession—from the political arena, to the world of celebrities, to everyday workplaces.

"This mass mobilization against sexual abuse, through an unprecedented wave of speaking out in conventional and social media, is eroding the two biggest barriers to ending sexual harassment in law and in life: the disbelief and trivializing dehumanization of its victims."[10] Finally, the world is beginning to change. Women are beginning to be heard and believed, rather than dismissed and devalued.

What does a correct reading of this passage tell you about yourself? Do you see yourself differently now?

---

9. The Hebrew Bible/Old Testament was originally written in Hebrew; the New Testament, in Greek.

10. MacKinnon, "#MeToo," para. 2.

*And the rib that the L*ORD *God had taken from the man he made into a woman and brought her to the man. Then the man said, "This at last is bone of my bones and flesh of my flesh."*

GENESIS 2:22–23

If there were ever a couple who epitomized the equality described in this passage, in which woman and man are bone of each other's bone and flesh of each other's flesh, it is Martin and Ruth Bader Ginsberg.

At the beginning of the film, *On the Basis of Sex*, RBG has just begun Harvard Law School. The year is 1956. At a welcoming dinner in his home, the Dean says, "Esteemed colleagues, ladies, this is only the sixth year women have had the privilege to earn a Harvard Law Degree. This little soirée is our way of saying welcome. My wife Helen and I are very glad all nine of you have joined us. Let us go around the table. Each of you ladies report who you are, where you're from, and why you're occupying a place at Harvard that could have gone to a man."[11]

That was like throwing a bucket of cold water on every woman in attendance. Nevertheless, two women did not hesitate to answer. The second speaker was immediately put down by the Dean who stated, "That's not a very good reason."[12]

After spilling her cutlery on the floor in nervousness, the young Ruth Bader Ginsberg took her turn. "I'm Ruth Ginsberg from Brooklyn." Prep school eyebrows were raised around the table. "Mrs. Ginsberg. My husband Marty is in the second-year class. I'm at Harvard to learn more about his work so I can be a more patient and understanding wife."[13] Every woman in attendance spewed laughter at her audacity, and this was just the beginning for Ruth Bader Ginsberg.

In this 1950s environment, Ruth's husband supported her physically, emotionally, and spiritually as she sought to live into who God created her to be within a patriarchal culture that did not value her as a woman. She supported her husband in every way as well.

11. Leder, *On the Basis of Sex*, Film.
12. Leder, *On the Basis of Sex*, Film.
13. Leder, *On the Basis of Sex*, Film.

This marriage of equals is depicted in God's original intent for Adam and Eve. Yet, it is the Fake News of women as inferior that has lived for centuries in the hearts and minds of women and men alike.

What would your life look like if this passage informed your self-image and relationships?

To the woman he (God) said . . . "your desire shall be for your
husband, and he shall rule over you."

GENESIS 3:16

I was six years old, wearing one of those petticoats that crinkled when you sat down, along with my best Mary Jane shoes, lace ankle socks, and Sunday hat. Attending church with my Southern Baptist grandparents was a treat. In the summer it could be hot, but the collective force of five hundred Jesus fans made the air just fine. Never mind that Jesus was portrayed with blond hair and blue eyes. This was the 1950s, when political correctness meant inviting the right politician's wife to your home for tea.

This morning, the preacher bellowed, "And your husband shall ruuuuuule over you!" I elbowed my grandmother and gave her a questioning look. "It's in the marriage vows. Obey your husband," she whispered. And, indeed, it was, but this was not what God intended.

What does God want for each of us? In creating male and female, God intends the woman to be an equal partner to the man, someone to whom he can relate as one human being to another. Significantly, the above statement from Genesis occurs as punishment after Adam and Eve eat of the forbidden fruit. It is part of the fallen order, not the created order. The traditional interpretation of the husband as the ruler of his wife is Fake News that has been historically misused to force wives to submit to their husbands, even in cases of abuse.

To "rule over" another person is to dominate them. The misreading of this statement has caused suffering throughout the ages and has sanctioned bullying behavior—in a marriage, in the workplace, in school—wherever men and women interact.

During one of her trademark heart-warming stories, Sarah Bessey writes, "Patriarchy is not God's dream for humanity. I'll say that again, louder, and I'll stand up beside our small bonfire and shout it out loud. I'll scare the starfish and the powerful alike: patriarchy is not God's dream for humanity. It never was; it never will be. Instead, in Christ and because of Christ, we are invited to *participate* in the Kingdom of God through redemptive movement—for both men and women—toward equality and freedom."[14]

Throughout the ages, God has been working to re-create each one of us and to restore right relationships among us that reflect the original intent of creation.

How might you participate in God's movement toward equality and freedom for you?

14. Bessey, *Jesus Feminist*, 14.

When God created humankind, he made them in the likeness of God.
Male and female he created them.

GENESIS 5:1–2

Just in case we missed the first creation account of male and female created simultaneously and as equals, it is repeated in the book of Genesis four chapters later. This account appears not once, but twice, yet most people have never heard of it.

In this creation account, there is nothing secondary about womankind. From the beginning of time, male and female are created in the likeness of God—from the beginning of time, in the Bible, the book most often quoted to put women "in their place." The selective remembering of woman as created second and therefore inferior helped lay the foundation for patriarchal systems still in place throughout the world.

Over fifty years after the United States passed the Equal Pay Act, American women still face significant gender wage gaps across the spectrum. According to a recent study by U.S. economists, the standard wage gap measured by the Census Bureau shows that a woman working full-time makes on average, 80.7 cents for every dollar earned by her male counterpart. This gap in pay varies widely, depending on location, race, and several other factors.[15]

In developing nations, the disparities are greater and more diverse. Only sixty percent of girls are enrolled in primary school and thirty percent in secondary school. Girls are two and a half times more likely to be out of school than boys in conflict-riddled countries. Globally, more than 750 million girls alive today were married before the age of eighteen, and at least 200 million women and girls worldwide have undergone female genital mutilation.[16]

Each statistic points to a value system in which women are regarded as inferior to men. The Bible stories we tell matter. The Bible stories women and men remember matter.

Could this creation story change the image you have of yourself? Could it help you claim the life of spiritual truth and fulfillment God desires for you?

15. Sheth et al., "7 charts," para. 4.
16. UN Women, "Facts and Figures," para. 2, 3, 10, 12.

Is there someone else you know who needs to hear this True News?

But Jesus said to them . . . "From the beginning of creation, God made them male and female."

MARK 10:5-6

The creation account in which male and female are created simultaneously as equals appears twice in the Hebrew Bible/Old Testament. Significantly, when Jesus chooses to speak of the creation of man and woman, he quotes from this account. This view of women as equal is consistent with Jesus' treatment of women throughout his life.

Unlike other rabbis of his time, Jesus healed women. He healed the woman with a flow of blood who was considered ritually unclean, he spoke to the Samaritan woman at the well who was not only a woman but a foreigner, he stood up for the woman taken in adultery, and he applauded Mary of Bethany for choosing to learn from him, an activity not permitted to women. Jesus had women disciples who traveled with him, and, after his resurrection, he chose to appear first to Mary Magdalene, making a significant statement of his value of women.

The belief that females are inferior to males because the Bible says it is so is soul-destroying Fake News that has led to the rise of a two-tiered system with women second, a system that has been in place for thousands of years and is still flourishing throughout the world.

This system has impacted the lives of both women and men in negative ways. When half the population is prevented from living into the person God created them to be, everyone loses. While progress has been made, particularly in first-world countries, much progress is yet to be realized.

Has this system impacted your life? How do you hear these words of Jesus?

"In the last days it will be," God declares, *"that I will pour out my Spirit on all flesh, and your sons and your daughters will prophesy."*

ACTS 2:17

I met Rachel Held Evans when she came to my community to lead a retreat. Pregnant with her second child, she asked her Twitter followers to pray for her during this, her last speaking engagement before giving birth. Many of her female followers chimed in with the promise of prayer and identification with her situation. That was Rachel—one of us.

One year later, at the age of thirty-seven, she was dead from unexpected brain seizures that led to brain swelling. The outpouring of grief at her untimely death was overwhelming. In *USA Today* Jonathan Merritt wrote, "But the reason a writer as young as Evans mattered to so many is that, religiously speaking, she was not just a writer. Evans was a prophet with a pen."[17]

Raised in the South as an evangelical Christian, Evans pointed out in her books, blogs, and social media posts that some of what the evangelical church taught was not based on sound biblical scholarship—particularly the church's position on women. To demonstrate the absurdity of some biblical statements about women, she lived for a year as women in the Bible were commanded to do—covering her head, calling her husband "master," even sleeping in a tent in her yard during her periods.[18]

Her chronicle of this year became *The New York Times* bestseller, *A Year of Biblical Womanhood*. No longer able to ignore her, male evangelical leaders challenged her in Twitter posts, often to find themselves coming up short in response to her quick mind and fearless ability to speak truth to power.

For you see, that's what prophets do. They speak truth to power, especially during times of marginalization and upheaval. As our Creator told us thousands of years ago, the gift of prophecy has been poured out on our daughters and our sons, and, as a result, many are living life more abundantly than ever before.

The Spirit is alive. The Spirit is moving. Can you feel it? Are you called to speak truth to power in your setting?

17. Merritt, "Rachel Held Evans," para. 2.
18. Evans, *A Year of Biblical Womanhood*.

Women should be silent in the churches. For they are not permitted to speak, but should be subordinate as the law also says.

1 CORINTHIANS 14:34–35

I do not permit a woman to teach or have authority over a man.

1 TIMOTHY 2:12

"Women must keep silent in church. They must never be in a leadership position anywhere. It says so, right here in the Bible!"

Not so fast. Is this what Paul meant by these words, or could they have a different meaning? As is the case with every verse of Scripture, we cannot take it out of context and assume we have the intended meaning.

Sitz im Leben is a German phrase that describes a method of biblical scholarship. It means "setting in life" and raises the question of context. What was the purpose of these words at the time they were written? Did Paul mean that women were not allowed to speak in church during his lifetime? For all time?

The belief that women are not permitted to speak in church based on the teachings of Paul is Fake News of the worst sort. Paul himself elevated women to positions of leadership. There is Junia, whom he named as an apostle; Phoebe, whom he named as a deacon and saint; Prisca, his equal partner in spreading the gospel. The common understanding of these texts today did not even apply in Paul's lifetime, much less in ours.

So, what did they mean? Most of Paul's letters were meant to address specific problems within a given community at a time in history. Earlier in this same letter, he told women *how* they were to pray and prophesy in public meetings. So, he clearly meant that women could function in this manner in his own day. His letter to Timothy is personal and deals with specific issues. Unfortunately, we don't know what they were. Nonetheless, given Paul's actions and his repeated words of commendation for women leaders, he did not mean for these words to be applied to all situations in his own day or in generations to come.

Does this change your view of Paul? Or does it change your view of the role of women today?

Racism

"If Obama weren't black he'd be a tour guide in Honolulu,
or he'd be teaching Saul Alinsky constitutional law."[1]
Rush Limbaugh

"I don't believe Rush Limbaugh has a racist bone in his body."[2]
Mike Pence

1. Spak, "Limbaugh," para. 2.
2. Nichols, "Trump Pick Pence," para. 18.

For in God's own image God made humankind.

GENESIS 9:6

"If only people would see me for the type of person I am and for the type of heart I have," Emma told me, as she stood there, slowly patting her heart.

Before attending seminary, I established a high-school equivalency program in a predominantly black community in Trenton, New Jersey. It was challenging for many of the students to travel to the local campus, so we brought the campus to their neighborhood. I learned a great deal in the five years I worked there.

Among other things, I learned that motherhood is the universal language. Regardless of where a mother lives, she wants the same opportunities for her children—an ability to grow up in a safe neighborhood, a good education, a promising future. In my privileged suburban life, I would sometimes hear disparaging remarks that were nothing less than Fake News about women on welfare not genuinely caring about their children or even themselves.

One morning, one of my homeless students was particularly agitated. I took Emma into another room to talk, where used clothing was stored for resale in the community. She stood there, amid musty boxes piled high, in clothes she had worn for two weeks. She told me over and over that someday people would not judge her by her outward appearance but would see her for the type of person she was and for the type of heart she had. "Emma has a good heart," she said, "if only people could see it." She just stood there patting her heart, repeating these words to me.

Each one of us is created in God's image—black, brown, and white; female and male; rich and poor; young and old; gay and straight; able and disabled. Anything we read that sets us up as different from one another or one as superior to the other is nothing less than soul-destroying Fake News.

What if everyone were treated as if they were made in the image of the Divine? How might our national dialogue be different? How would this affect the prevalence of racial profiling today?

[C]Then she [Hagar] went and sat down opposite him [the boy] a good way off . . . And as she sat opposite him, she lifted up her voice and wept. And God heard the voice of the boy.

GENESIS 21:16–17

In the book of Genesis, Hagar was enslaved by Abraham and Sarah. Since Sarah was barren, Hagar was informed that she must bear Abraham's child. Having no say in the matter, Hagar conceives and bears a son who is named Ishmael. Subsequently, Sarah becomes pregnant by Abraham and gives birth to Isaac. After Hagar has served her purpose in bearing a son, Sarah severely mistreats her, and Hagar runs away to the desert with Ishmael.

Womanist theologian Delores S. Williams writes, "Hagar becomes the first female in the Bible to liberate herself from oppressive power structures. Though the law prescribes harsh punishment for runaway slaves, she takes the risk rather than endure more brutal treatment by Sarai."[3]

Today the abuse of the descendants of enslaved people in the U.S. is increasing. African Americans are more likely to be shot by police in the United States than their white peers. While the U.S. population is 13 percent black, 39 percent of all people killed by U.S. police while *not* attacking are black.[4]

On the night Oscar Grant died, he was out with friends celebrating New Year's Eve in Oakland, California. At approximately two am he was dragged off a train, cooperative and unarmed, telling his friends to obey the police. "That did nothing to save Oscar Grant. Within minutes, without cause, a police officer would shoot him in the back, execution-style."[5] The event was captured on multiple official videos, as well as on cell phone cameras.

In seeking to understand the lives of Hagar in the Bible and African Americans like Oscar Grant, Botham Jean, and Atatiana Jefferson, we will more fully understand both ourselves and the society in which we live. Professor Clarice J. Martin writes, "African-American autobiographies are . . . a 'mirror of white deeds.' If

3. Williams, *Sisters in the Wilderness*, 19.
4. Lopez, "There are Huge Racial Disparities," graph 1.
5. Amnesty International, "Another year," para. 1.

autobiography links both history and literature, objective fact and subjective awareness, then it serves to remove fully the mask that seeks to camouflage the ugly reality of the continuing legacy of slavery and the ubiquitous and pervasive expressions of racism."[6]

What one action could you take to remove the mask surrounding one of the pervasive expressions of racism today?

6. Martin, "Black Theodicy," loc. 405.

Say therefore to the Israelites, "I am the LORD, and I will free you from
the burdens of the Egyptians and deliver you from slavery to them.
I will redeem you with an outstretched arm and with mighty acts of
judgment."

EXODUS 6:6

When God commands Moses to deliver the Israelites from slavery
in Egypt, our Creator speaks from within a burning bush in the wilderness. What an incredible sight Moses encounters, a thorn bush
engulfed in flames that burns but is not consumed. Most of us have
never seen a thorn bush, but, as a shepherd, Moses sees them every
day, much as we might see an oak tree. Imagine walking out of your
home to see a tree on fire, but with leafy green branches waving in the
wind. I don't know about you, but that would get my attention. Then
imagine hearing a voice coming out of the tree claiming to be God.

This startling experience is what happens to Moses. After answering the call of God from the burning bush, Moses goes on to
lead the people of Israel out of slavery in Egypt, through the parted
waters of the Red Sea, and toward the Promised Land.

Why does God call him and why does he respond affirmative-
ly? Because God sees the misery of his enslaved children, hears their
cries, knows their utter desperation, and acts. God does whatever
it takes to get Moses' attention and Moses responds. Immediately.

The tragic plight of enslaved people throughout the centuries
has been one of abuse, misery and abject injustice. Here in the book
of Exodus, God, once and for all time, sides with the enslaved—not
the rulers, not the oppressors. The enslaved.

The *Slave Bible*, originally published in London in 1807, de-
leted passages like this one. Completely. For they tell a message
of liberation, hope, and freedom for enslaved peoples. In fact, the
Slave Bible omitted ninety percent of the Hebrew Bible/Old Testament and fifty percent of the New Testament.[7]

The Slave Bible was the ultimate Fake News, deliberate pro-
paganda to aid an evil system. The disastrous effects of this kind
of Fake News are apparent in America today. People of color still

7. Museum, "The Slave Bible," para. 1.

struggle against institutionalized racism that permeates every facet of their lives.

While Moses is described as seeing a real burning bush, there are figurative burning bushes all around us in daily news accounts of discrimination. Can you see them? How might you be a Moses?

While they were at Hazeroth, Miriam and Aaron spoke against Moses
because of the Cushite woman whom he had married (for he had indeed
married a Cushite woman) . . . Then the LORD *came down in a pillar*
of cloud, and stood at the entrance of the tent, and called Aaron and
Miriam; and both came forward . . . And the anger of the LORD *was*
kindled against them, and God departed.

NUMBERS 12:1, 5, 9

As a Hebrew, Moses is expected to marry a Hebrew, yet instead he marries outside his race. Moses' second wife Zipporah is a Cushite, an Ethiopian, and therefore African. Miriam and Aaron, Moses' sister and brother, speak out against the marriage and are severely reprimanded by God. We are told, "the anger of the LORD was kindled against them." Strong language. Our Creator was not only displeased but angry.

Separation of the races based on the belief that "this is what God has ordained" is Fake News that has led to the existence of slavery in the United States and the ongoing unequal treatment of people based on race. When Scripture was misused to support the existence of slavery, this passage was most certainly ignored.

In fact, it was ignored for centuries. While the U.S. Supreme Court ruled that laws prohibiting interracial marriage were unconstitutional in 1967, such laws remained in effect in several states. The last law in the U.S. officially prohibiting interracial marriage between blacks and whites was not repealed until the year 2000 in the state of Alabama.[8] Prior to that time, married interracial couples could be arrested and were considered felons, depending on the state in which they lived. How ironic that a leading biblical savior was married to an African woman.

Such laws were far from Jesus' injunction, "You shall love your neighbor as yourself" (Matthew 22:39). Not neighbors whose skin color matches our own, but all neighbors. Not neighbors who share our religious beliefs, but all neighbors. Not neighbors who have the same sexual orientation as ours, but all neighbors.

---

8. "Interracial Relationships that Changed History," para. 2.

How might history be different if it were widely acknowledged that Moses, one of the saviors of the Hebrew people, was married to an African?

Ebed-melech the Ethiopian, a eunuch in the king's house, heard that they had put Jeremiah into the cistern. The king happened to be sitting at the Benjamin Gate, So Ebed-melech left the king's house and spoke to the king, "My LORD king, these men have acted wickedly in all they did to the prophet Jeremiah by throwing him into the cistern to die there of hunger, for there is no bread left in the city." Then the king commanded Ebed-melech the Ethiopian, "Take three men with you from here, and pull the prophet Jeremiah up from the cistern before he dies." So Ebed-melech took the men with him and went to the house of the king, to a wardrobe of the storehouse, and took from there old rags and worn-out clothes, which he let down to Jeremiah in the cistern by ropes. Then Ebed-melech the Ethiopian said to Jeremiah, "Just put the rags and clothes between your armpits and the ropes." Jeremiah did so. Then they drew Jeremiah up by the ropes and pulled him out of the cistern. And Jeremiah remained in the court of the guard.

JEREMIAH 38:7–13

Just as Zipporah, Moses' wife, played a role in salvation history, other Africans were also pivotal in the redemptive activity of God. Ebed-Melech, an Ethiopian, saved the life of Jeremiah, who is recognized as a prophet in the Jewish, Christian, and Islamic faiths.

Known as the "weeping prophet," Jeremiah prophesized that Jerusalem would be handed over to the Babylonian army. Concerned that Jeremiah was discouraging his soldiers, King Zedekiah ordered his officials to kill him. So, they threw him into a cistern with the intent of starving him to death.

Only one person had the courage to confront the king over his evil actions—Ebed-Melech. The king changed his mind and ordered Ebed-Melech to pull Jeremiah out of the cistern. By being willing to risk his own life, Ebed-Melech saved the life of one of the major prophets in the history of Israel.

As has repeatedly occurred with women who had active roles in salvation history, the African Ebed-Melech is seldom mentioned or is referred to merely as "the Cushite," a biblical name referencing the peoples of northeast Africa.

Cain Hope Felder has written, "Black people are not only frequently mentioned [in the Bible], but are also mentioned in ways that are favorable in terms of acknowledging their actual and potential role in the salvation history of Israel."[9] Felder is clear that racial and ethnic diversity is part of biblical heritage, dispelling Eurocentric biblical interpretations that persist today. His research also shows that blacks were in King David's army as described in Second Samuel.[10]

It is past time for the Fake News of a Eurocentric biblical understanding to end. In the Bible, blacks fought in the army, saved people's lives, as did Ebed-Melech, ruled countries, as did the Queen of Sheba, and were married to well-known saviors, as was Zipporah.

How might history have been different if this True News had been taught?

9. Felder, ed., *Stony the Road,* 136.

10. Silliman, "Died: Cain Hope Felder," para. 7.

If a slave has taken refuge with you, do not hand them over to their master.

DEUTERONOMY 23:15

In the pre-Civil War South, an enslaved man named Tice Davids ran away from his master. After an arduous hair-raising trek, he made it to the Ohio River opposite Ripley, Ohio, the home of Rev. John Rankin, a well-known abolitionist and Presbyterian minister. Rankin lived in a house with his family on the banks of the Ohio and ran a well-established Underground Railroad, which put his life and the life of his family at constant risk. Within a month of an attack on his family, he wrote the following published letter:

> REVEREND JOHN RANKIN, RIPLEY, OHIO, 1841
> Thus have I been attacked at midnight with fire and weapons of death, and nothing but the good providence of God has preserved my property from flames and myself and family from violence and death. And why? Have I wronged anyone? No, but I am an ABOLITIONIST. I do not recognize the slaveholder's right to the flesh and blood and souls of men and women. For this I must be proscribed, my property burnt, and my life put in jeopardy! Now I desire all men to know that I am not to be deterred from what I believe to be my duty by fire and sword. I also wish all to know that I feel it my duty to defend my HOME to the very uttermost, and that it is as much a duty to shoot the midnight assassin in his attacks as it is to pray.[11]

Rev. Rankin never wavered in his conviction, never turned away one enslaved person on the run. One night, Tice crouched on the riverbank, not sure when or how to cross the river from Kentucky into Ohio and freedom. The man who owned him was following him in a small boat. Tice was at great risk and he knew it. Suddenly he heard one of the sounds the Rankins commonly used to alert slaves— a birdcall or a ringing bell—that let him know there was someone there to help him on the other side of the river if he could make it across.

11. Rankin, published letter, quoted in Hagedorn, *Beyond the River,* loc. 121.

A man named Siebert, who wrote about the system used by the Rankins and neighboring abolitionists, recorded this method of escape. It was designed to help guide the runaways safely to shore. In addition to birdcalls and bells, the Rankins used a light in their window. Their house sat on a bluff overlooking the river. This light was legendary and became a beacon of hope and visual guide for many miles out on dark nights.

As the story goes, Tice saw the Rankin light on the bluff and then swam underwater to it, baffling the slaveholder in the skiff, who reported that Tice "just disappeared into something like an underground railroad."[12]

"If a slave has taken refuge with you, do not hand them over to their master." I do not doubt that Rev. John Rankin, from whom I am honored to be descended, took these words to heart as he risked his life night after night to protect the enslaved children of God entrusted to his care.

12. Tobin and Dobard, *Hidden in Plain View*, 61–62.

Rescue the weak and the needy; deliver them from the hand of the wicked.

PSALM 82:4

"At the time of my victimization I didn't know what human trafficking was, but I knew that being a person of color didn't make it any easier. Many of my buyers, both male and female, were white," shared a young woman of color who was rescued from trafficking by the Connecticut Human Anti-trafficking Response Team.[13]

The belief that slavery no longer exists is an insidious form of Fake News that allows human slavery to flourish. Today there are more slaves than at any other time in history. The U.S. State Department estimates that there are as many as forty-seven million slaves in the world today. To put this in perspective, there were approximately four million slaves in the United States in 1860.

Human traffickers globally net thirty-two billion dollars a year in profits, more than Google, Starbucks, and Nike combined. Human trafficking is second only to the illegal drug trade in revenue. Yet most people are unaware that it is flourishing today, right here in America, right under our noses. Forced labor and child labor, sex trafficking, child sex trafficking, and involuntary domestic servitude are all aspects of modern-day slavery, many of which are racially motivated.

It is painful to realize that human trafficking occurs all around us and yet we do not see it. Would you be surprised to learn that the highest volume of trafficking in the U.S. occurs at high profile sporting events? I was. The reality is that the seamier side of the Super Bowl and the underbelly of every major sporting event in the United States are seldom mentioned. Not on the nightly news. Not in most newspaper reports. Not in most online venues.

"One Super Bowl after another after another has shown itself to be one of the largest events in the world where the cruelty of human trafficking goes on for several weeks," said U.S. Rep. Chris Smith, R-N.J., co-chairman of the House Anti-human trafficking Caucus.[14]

13. Young et al., "Let's Talk About Race," para. 6.
14. Zezima and Henry, "N.J. works to curb," para. 3.

Human trafficking is a spiritual matter, a justice matter, a "love your neighbor as yourself matter," and it is a matter of life and death for the young girls and boys whose lives are forever altered for the pleasure and callousness of those willing to pay for the use of their bodies for sex, labor, or servitude.

What steps can we take to change this abysmal reality? To begin with, we can take off the blinders and see what is happening in our own country and in our own communities. Second, we can support one of the nonprofits that fight this modern-day scourge.[15] Third, we can buy from Fair Trade Certified organizations that can and do make a difference.[16]

We can all do something, no matter how small. What contribution might you make to help rescue the weak and needy and deliver them from the hand of the wicked?

15. See DurgaTreeInternational.org and Love146.org.
16. For a list of Slave Free companies, see EndSlaveryNow.org.

But let justice roll down like waters, and righteousness like an ever-flowing stream.

AMOS 5:24–26

Have you ever had a dream you were willing to die for? Have you ever had a dream that would transform an entire nation? Have you ever had a dream that someday, somehow, justice would roll down like waters and righteousness like an ever-flowing stream for you and all your loved ones?

In 1968, the Rev. Dr. Martin Luther King Jr. boldly proclaimed that he dared to dream such a dream. A dream that ignited the imagination and stirred the souls of many. A dream that evoked fear and hate in many others.

I'll never forget the day King was assassinated in my home state of Tennessee. The African American students in my high school staged a peaceful sit-in in the cafeteria while some of my white classmates derided them for their actions. I'll never forget the shame I felt over the color of my skin. I'll never forget the looks on the faces of my black sisters and brothers who sat there in reverent silence. Yet I had no idea what I could do to make a difference.

Then one day years later, our daughter came home from school with an announcement about an outreach ministry in a predominantly black community in Trenton, New Jersey. Her school was looking for people to tutor adults there once a week. I left the announcement in a pile of paperwork and forgot about it. Several weeks later another announcement came, then another.

Gradually I realized there was something God wanted to teach me in Trenton, if only I would take the first step. But I was afraid. Afraid of people I didn't know and afraid of what I might find out about myself if I did go. Then I remembered the faces of my classmates that day in Tennessee, so many years before. And I remembered the man who dared to dream, the man who started the march to freedom. And finally, I picked up my feet and started to march with him.

My perspective on the reality of life in America for all God's children was never the same after that. I soon realized that the blinders I wore were more comfortable than the truth they hid.

And what is the truth? A recent Federal Reserve survey reveals an appalling economic reality in the U.S. today for African Americans and Hispanics. "The median net worth of African American households in 2013 was only $11,000 and $13,700 for Latino households—one-thirteenth and one-tenth, respectively, of the median net worth of white households, which stood at $141,900."[17]

Please. Reread these statistics and let this reality sink in. Can you envision the people behind the numbers? How is their life the same as or different than yours?

17. Center, "How Predatory Debt," para. 11.

Paul . . . To all God's beloved in Rome . . . "We know that the whole creation has been groaning in labor pains until now; and not only the creation, but we ourselves who have the first fruits of the Spirit, groan inwardly while we wait for adoption, the redemption of our bodies.

ROMANS 1:1, 7, 8:22–23

As Grand Dragon of the Ku Klux Klan, Ken Parker marched in the 2017 Unite the Right rally in Charlottesville, Virginia. A few months after the rally, he noticed his African American neighbor grilling out by a swimming pool near his apartment. Not knowing the man was a pastor, he approached the neighbor, William McKinnon III, to ask some questions. The pastor suggested they talk further, which they did, and he ended up inviting Parker to his church on Easter Sunday.

Parker accepted the invitation and later renounced his involvement with the KKK and neo-Nazis. After testifying about his past supremacist activities, he was astonished to find himself embraced, not judged, by the principally African American congregation. Two months later, he wore a different kind of robe and was baptized by Pastor McKinnon in the Atlantic Ocean.[18]

In the above passage, Paul describes the entire created order groaning in labor, awaiting the birth of God's reign on earth. Yet, until we accept that our Creator loves us unconditionally and loves our neighbor equally, creation will continue to groan in labor.

I do not doubt that our Divine Mother was groaning in the birth pangs of labor, waiting for Ken Parker to free himself from the bonds of the Fake News that his white skin made him superior to those of other races, waiting for Ken to see his Creator in the face of those he hated. Each of us yearns for a community of people to love us. Unfortunately, some people choose the wrong community.

By the grace of God, this pastor and his church were able to reach a child of God who so desperately needed to be saved from himself. Could someone be waiting for you to reach out to them? What step might you take?

18. Franco and Radford, "Ex-KKK member," para. 16, 21, 23.

*There is One lawgiver and judge who is able to save and to destroy. So
who then are you to judge your neighbor?*

JAMES 4:12

Esteemed ancestors are immortalized in oil portraits that adorn the
walls of many homes in Charleston, South Carolina. The portrait of
an African American man with a curious look on his face hangs in
a quaint downtown restaurant. So, I asked about it.

"Ah, yes. Look at it closely. And be sure to see the portrait in
the entryway." In the entrance nearby is a full-length portrait of the
same man in topcoat and hat with a meringue pie in one hand and
a whip in the other. Which one of these objects a person will receive
in the afterlife depends on how they treat their neighbors in this life.

The artist, John Carroll Doyle, describes his subject in "The
Coachman" as a mythical black carriage driver who takes us on
our journey into the afterlife. Doyle writes, "He smiles a Cheshire
cat grin as if to say, 'Hey, cousin, it's you, not me, that's responsible
for your fate.' In one hand he holds a bullwhip for those who have
conveniently detached themselves from their conscience, becoming strangers to their souls. In his other hand, for those of us who
have been good, a cream pie awaits, for a joyful party that will last
for Eternity."[19]

I see something deeper in Doyle's painting. The carriage
driver's self-satisfied grin conveys to me that a person's place in the
afterlife depends especially on how they treat their black neighbors
in this life.

During the Transatlantic Slave Trade, approximately forty
percent of Africans brought to the United States to be sold and
enslaved passed through the Charleston Harbor. "This place is absolutely central to telling the story of slavery," said Bernard Powers,
a professor of history at the College of Charleston.[20]

Today, in the heart of that city stands this quiet but clear statement of both equality and judgment. All people are indeed equal in
the eyes of God, and yes, our Creator will judge us based on how we
treat our neighbor. This memorable painting speaks deeply to me

19. Doyle, "The Coachman," para. 1.
20. Hicks, "Slavery in Charleston," para. 15, 16.

that the judge at the end of time will not be an old white man with a beard, as God is often artistically portrayed, but a black man.

What if our Creator were depicted as an immigrant, an African, Hispanic, or Native American? What if our Creator were depicted wearing a Star of David or a hijab? Would this change your image of that group of people? Your actions toward them?

Heterosexism

"AIDS is not just God's punishment for homosexuals;
it is God's punishment for the society that tolerates
homosexuals."[1]

The Rev. Jerry Falwell Sr.

"Tyler Clementi, student outed as gay on internet,
jumps to his death."[2]

The Guardian

1. Morford, "The Sad Quotable Jerry," para. 3.
2. Pilkington, "Tyler Clementi," headline.

*The two angels came to Sodom in the evening, and Lot is sitting in the
gateway of Sodom. When Lot saw them . . . he said, "Please, my LORDS,
turn aside to your servant's house and spend the night . . . so they
turned aside to him and entered the house; and he made them a feast,
and baked unleavened bread, and they ate. But before they lay down,
the men of the city . . . surrounded the house; and they called to Lot,
"Where are the men who came to you tonight? Bring them out to us, so
that we may know them." Lot went out of the door to the men, shut the
door after him, and said, "I beg you my brothers, do not act so wickedly.
Look, I have two daughters who have not known a man; let me bring
them out to you, and do to them as you please; only do nothing to these
men, for they have come under the shelter of my roof."*

GENESIS 19:1–11

This passage has a long and misunderstood history. Clearly what
is related here is sinful— a group of local men demanding "to
know," or to have sexual relations with, two male strangers who
have entered their town. That is the first abomination, demanding
as a group to rape strangers, regardless of their gender. The second
occurs when Lot offers his two virgin daughters instead of the two
men. This is a paternal sin that should be remembered for all time.
Yet, it has been ignored throughout history.

Significantly, Lot's reason for refusing to send out the two men
is not that they are male, it is that they are guests in his home. "Do
nothing to these men, for they have come under the shelter of my
roof." The sin here in Lot's view is that the villagers are seeking to
violate his hospitality.

How strange this may seem to us today. Yet hospitality was
central in the life of first-century Jewish people. Hospitality was
considered a moral duty all over the Ancient Near East.

Not once in this passage does Lot even allude to homosexuality. Not once in the two occasions when Jesus mentions Sodom and
Gomorrah does he mention homosexuality. Instead, Jesus references the lack of hospitality as the sin. In the gospels of Matthew
and Luke, Jesus is clear.[3] The sin of Sodom is being inhospitable.

---

3. Matthew 10:11–15, Luke 10:8–12.

In the gospel of Matthew, when Jesus sends his apostles out to proclaim the good news, he tells them, "Whatever town or village you enter, find out who in it is worthy, and stay there until you leave. As you enter the house, greet it. If the house is worthy, let your peace come upon it; but if it is not worthy, let your peace return to you. If anyone will not welcome you or listen to your words, shake off the dust from your feet as you leave that house or town. Truly I tell you, it will be more tolerable for the land of Sodom and Gomorrah on the day of judgment than for that town" (Matt 10:11–15).

The sin of Sodom and Gomorrah in Jesus' view is lack of hospitality. The prevalent view that the sin of Sodom is homosexuality is major Fake News.

Does an understanding of the context of this oft-quoted passage change your view of the Bible? Or does it change your view of yourself or your loved one?

If a man lies with a male as with a woman, both of them have committed an abomination; they shall be put to death; their blood is upon them.

LEVITICUS 20:13

In a memorable episode of *The West Wing*, a journalist who believes homosexuality is an abomination questions the U.S. President. The President, played by Martin Sheen, responds by wanting to know a fair price for his daughter, because Exodus 21:7 sanctions selling her into slavery. He wants to know further if he should kill his Chief of Staff himself or call the police because he works on the Sabbath, forbidden in Exodus 35:2.[4]

Such questions point out the difficulty in interpreting the Bible literally. William Sloane Coffin wrote that those who do so are not biblical literalists, but selective literalists who cite only those passages that affirm a particular belief.[5] This selective literalism is glaringly obvious in passages like this one regarding homosexuality, which are quoted to the exclusion of others.

To understand them correctly, it is best to view these words in the original Hebrew in which they were written. Two different Hebrew words are used here; *ish* which means "man" and *zakhar* which means "male." This is a clue that the passage may in fact not be about two ordinary men engaging in sexual relations with one another, and, certainly, that it does not refer to a loving relationship between two committed men.

Ninety percent of the time, the rarely used Hebrew word *zakhar* designates a man or male animal dedicated to a deity for a sacred function. Thus, it is highly likely that this passage was meant to forbid men from visiting male prostitutes who served Canaanite deities. To further support this interpretation, the word for "abomination" is used most often in relation to idolatry.[6]

In *The Bible Doesn't Say That*, Hebrew scholar Dr. Joel Hoffman writes of this passage, "Some people . . . interpret it as referring to homosexuality in general, though it does not. Some

4. Glaser, *For the Bible Tells*, 31.
5. Coffin, *Credo*, 159.
6. Gerig, "The Clobber Passages," para. 5.

people even go a step further, claiming that Leviticus denounces homosexuality as a sin. But while it condemns certain behavior, it doesn't call it a 'sin.'"[7]

Can this understanding make a difference in your own life? Is there someone with whom you are meant to share this True News?

7. Hoffman, *The Bible Doesn't Say*, 244.

But now thus says the LORD . . . "I have called you by name, you are mine."

ISAIAH 43:1

There is so much to love about this passage. It can be comforting when we need comfort, empowering when we need empowerment, instructive when we need instruction.

I've never met anyone who didn't need comfort at some time in their life, from a simple bad day to a life-altering tragedy. When we find ourselves in such situations, we can rest in the knowledge that our Creator has called us by name and knows us personally. We belong. What an antidote for loneliness.

Empowerment? You bet. When we believe in our hearts that we matter enough to God, the Creator of the universe, to be named and to belong to the Divine, what can be more empowering?

Instructive? Ah, there's the rub. Many of us go through life not believing we need instruction, believing that we have all the answers. Then along comes the prevalence of news that is deliberately misleading, and we suddenly find ourselves on shaky ground. Can we believe what we read any more? What is the truth?

What if we read the news with this passage in mind? It doesn't say, "I have called some by name and not others." There are no qualifiers here. "You" is the universal "you." "You" includes gay and straight, black and white, Hispanic and Asian, rich and poor, old and young, male and female. "You" includes each one of God's children created in the image of God.

No one is excluded. Jacqueline Bussie writes, "One day . . . I saw an engraved woodcarving above a church door. It said EXCLUDE NO ONE. If God's love had a Twitter handle, this would be it. I vow to do my best to follow the love advice of @ExcludeNoOne."[8]

In the latest news story, is everyone being treated equally? Is any person or group of people being denigrated, treated like second-class citizens? If so, I would assert that it is not the True News as proclaimed throughout Scripture. It does not represent the abundant life God has in mind for each and every one of us.

"I have called you by name. You are mine." Rest in those words.

---

8. Bussie, *Love Without Limits,* loc. 94.

When you pass through the waters, I will be with you; and through the rivers, they shall not overwhelm you; when you walk through fire you shall not be burned . . . For I am the LORD your God.

ISAIAH 43:2–3

This passage of comfort is clear. Our Creator is with us in the darkest moments of our lives, when water is threatening to engulf us, and fire is tickling our toes. How easy it is to forget this when we are in the thick of it, when we may feel as if God has abandoned us. But God tells us, "I will be with you."

Significantly, there are no qualifiers here. God will be with you, and you, and you. The Divine Energy that gives life to all creation will be with you whether you are gay or straight; black, white, or brown; immigrant or citizen; female or male; Jewish or Muslim or Buddhist or Christian or spiritual but not religious. Our Creator is with you whether you are a believer or not. No one is outside the reach of God's loving embrace.

Then why do we sometimes live our lives as if some are "in" and some are "out?" As if some are more worthy than others, superior to others? Such thinking is Fake News and has no place in the natural order as God created it to be. Yet this belief has dominated history; gays, lesbians, bisexuals, and transgender persons still do not have equal choices and chances in America.

Today in the state of Texas "you can be fired for being gay. You can be denied a home for being gay. You can be barred from adopting a child who needs a loving family because you're gay."[9] Lesbians and gays are still physically attacked, and there are places they do not feel safe. As a result, many keep quiet about who they are. In addition, LGBT youth are three and a half times more likely to attempt suicide than their heterosexual peers; transgender youth are nearly six times as likely to attempt suicide as their heterosexual peers.[10]

In his landmark book in the evangelical world, *God and the Gay Christian*, Matthew Vines writes, "Jesus's test is simple: If something bears bad fruit, it cannot be a good tree. And if something

9. O'Rourke, Tweet.
10. Carroll, *"LGBT youth,"* para. 2, 3.

bears good fruit, it cannot be a bad tree."[11] In an interview, he goes on to state, "The consequences of the evangelical church's categorical rejection of same-sex relationships have been anything but good: higher likelihoods of depression, illegal drug use, relational brokenness, and suicide. These are all red flags that opposing same-sex marriage isn't the best understanding of Scripture."[12] Amen. It is well past time for this traditional understanding to change.

Deep down inside, is there a group of people to whom you feel superior? If there is, could you envision them in the Divine embrace, envision our Creator walking through fire with them and saving them from rising waters? What would this say about God's view of that person?

How might it transform your very being? How might this passage transform the self-understanding of our gay and lesbian brothers and sisters?

11. Vines, *God and the Gay Christian*, 14.
12. Amazon, "Q and A."

When David had finished speaking to Saul, the soul of Jonathan was bound to the soul of David, and Jonathan loved him as his own soul … Then Jonathan made a covenant with David, because he loved him as his own soul. Jonathan stripped himself of the robe that he was wearing, and gave it to David, and his armor, and even his sword and his bow and his belt.

1 SAMUEL 18:1–4

"I am distressed for you my brother Jonathan; greatly beloved were you to me; your love to me was wonderful, passing the love of women."

2 SAMUEL 1:26

The love between the man who would become King David and Jonathan, the son of King Saul, has been stunningly portrayed within Scripture and stunningly ignored for centuries. Their souls were bound to one another. Jonathan, a prince, loved the ruddy shepherd boy David "as his own soul." Upon meeting David, Jonathan immediately gives him his most coveted possessions—his robe, his armor, even his sword, bow, and belt. He literally disarms himself, becoming vulnerable and defenseless before a man he has just met.

Can you imagine such an initial meeting with one man immediately giving the other his prized gold watch, family ring, and most coveted hunting gun? It would be highly unusual. Following this meeting, David becomes so popular that King Saul fears he will try to take over his throne. As a result, he makes plans to kill him.

Fearing for his life, David escapes; then he and Jonathan meet in secret. Jonathan vows to stand up for David before his father and does so one night at dinner. King Saul's response is strong and clear when he states, "You son of a perverse, rebellious woman! Do I not know that you have chosen [David] the son of Jesse to your own shame and to the shame of your mother's nakedness?" (1 Samuel 20:30). Instead of accepting his son's reality as God's will, Saul blames it on Jonathan's mother.

"Many gay men have experienced dinner conversations that sounded very similar to this one. They made the mistake of talking about their lover at the table, and their father became furious. More often than not, the blame goes first to the mother, who was "too soft," or "too harsh," or who "perverted" her son somehow. Then the father turns his anger toward the son: 'Can't you see how you're shaming the whole family?'"[13]

When King Saul and Jonathan are killed in battle, David grieves Jonathan's death with the grief of a lover. In doing so, he pens these words for all to see the depth of his love. "Greatly beloved were you to me; your love to me was wonderful, passing the love of women."

"I have always loved this story and see it as a beacon hidden in plain sight," shared the Rev. Burl Salmon, colleague and friend. He and his husband, Bob Henkel, chose the story of Jonathan and David to be read at their October 2015 wedding ceremony in Natchez, Mississippi. May the story of Jonathan and David continue to give our gay and lesbian brothers and sisters the positive biblical role model of a loving couple they so deserve. May their love be a shining example to those who still await acceptance by their family, society, or religious community.

Who do you know who needs to hear this True News of the love between David and Jonathan?

13. Would Jesus Discriminate? *"David Loved Jonathan,"* para. 11.

". . ." said Jesus, referring to his gay and lesbian neighbors.

ALL OF THE NEW TESTAMENT

No, this is not a misprint. There are no words that can be placed between these quotation marks. Why? Because Jesus never uttered one word about gays or lesbians. Not one. No words of condemnation, rebuke, or reprimands. No admonitions to change lifestyle, behavior, or orientation. Yet today this issue consumes the Christian church and, in some cases, has led to schism. It remains an issue within Judaism and Islam as well.

Walter Wink addresses this misuse of Scripture in his book, *Homosexuality and Christian Faith.* I would like to suggest that his words can inform all people, not just Christians.

Wink writes that, after careful study, many people have now realized "how mute the Bible is regarding a committed homosexual union between mature adults. The Bible's mere seven mentions of homosexual behavior—what gay and lesbian Christians have called "the clobber passages"—include some lines of the Leviticus purity code (which includes many rules from which Jesus liberates Christians), some sentences in Corinthians and Timothy that many Greek biblical scholars say referred to men exploiting boys, and a passage in Romans. Although Jesus affirmed marriage, he spoke no recorded words about homosexual behavior . . ."[14]

Nonetheless, this reality does not stop people in influential political and religious positions today from declaring that there is only one acceptable Christian understanding regarding homosexuality, that of condemnation. It does not stop some traditions from endorsing conversion therapy, which seeks to change a person's sexual orientation. It does not stop an extremist group from demonstrating with hate signs at the funerals of high-profile gay and lesbian people. The barrage of negative statements about gays and lesbians, touted as the word of God, is Fake News of the highest order.

Jesus did not utter one word about homosexuality. Does this change your view of what Scripture teaches us on this subject? Why has the belief that Jesus condemned homosexuals been allowed to flourish for centuries?

Are you called to share this True News with others?

14. Wink, *Homosexuality,* 68.

Anti-Semitism

"Jews will not replace us! Jews will not replace us!"[1]

White Supremacists, 2017 Rally
Charlottesville, Virginia

1. Rosenberg, "Jews," para. 6.

As for me, this is my covenant with you: You shall be the ancestor
of a multitude of nations. No longer shall your name be Abram, but
your name shall be Abraham; for I have made you the ancestor of a
multitude of nations. I will make you exceedingly fruitful; and I will
make nations of you.

GENESIS 17:4–6

Who are the nations and people descended from Abraham? Jews, Christians, and Muslims. Abraham and Sarah's son Isaac became the ancestor of Jews and Christians, while Abraham and Hagar's son Ishmael became the ancestor of Muslims. The value of this common heritage cannot be overstated.

Emeritus Chief Rabbi Jonathan Sacks writes, "Jews, Christians, and Muslims disagree on many things, but they also agree on some, not least in tracing their descent, spiritual or biological, from Abraham . . . Going back to the roots of biblical monotheism we may find, to our surprise, a theological basis for respect for difference, based not on relativism but on the concept of covenant."[2]

While on pilgrimage in Israel, I was reminded of this powerful connection between people who have been at war with one another throughout history. Heartbreaking stories of the bombing of synagogues, churches, and mosques continue to bleed from daily headlines.

Praying at the Western Wall in Jerusalem can be a sacred, life-changing experience. Separated from the men, women pray in silence or weep, some clutching their Torah, some with both hands on the wall. I join them. Slipping my carefully written prayer into a crevice, I place my hands on the wall beside theirs. Through a partition, I hear the Jewish men chanting, praying, their voices rising to their Creator as some sway back and forth, back and forth. The enforced separation of the sexes is uncomfortable to me, but I stay. And I pray.

Over the din of raised voices, I hear another prayer magnified by a speaker, the Muslim call to prayer—another kind of chanting mingling with the chants of my Jewish brothers next door. A

2. Sacks, *Dignity of Difference*, viii.

cacophony of voices all praising the same Creator, all praying, beseeching, asking for . . . what?

In a few moments, I hear a sound more familiar to me, the echo of church bells resounding through the air, pealing sounds of joy and praise and new life. The sounds know no borders, no boundaries, no walls. They soar above them all, dancing together in their praise of the one true God.

Listen to what these co-mingled sounds of praise and glory are saying to all of us in our fragmented world today. Listen.

Six days later, Jesus took with him Peter and James and John, and led them up a high mountain apart, by themselves. And he was transfigured before them, and his clothes became dazzling white ... Then Peter said to Jesus, "Rabbi, it is good for us to be here."

MARK 9:2–5

In the New Testament, everyone from Peter to Judas to Mary Magdalene addresses Jesus as "rabbi." While Jesus was never part of the official temple leadership, he was considered a rabbi because of his ministry of teaching. In the first century, the title "rabbi" merely indicated that a Jewish man was a wise teacher.

Everyone who calls themselves Christian worships a crucified and risen Jew. How quickly people forget that not only was Jesus a Jew, he was a Middle Eastern male. For centuries, artistic renderings of Jesus were of a light brown haired, blue-eyed European man. Such paintings are nothing other than artistic Fake News, which has made it much easier for generations of people the world over to forget who Jesus really was.

Such renderings have not only aided anti-Semitic beliefs but have also caused them to flourish throughout history, with a disturbing resurgence today. The white supremacists who marched in Charlottesville, West Virginia in 2017 continuously shouted, "Jews will not replace us! Jews will not replace us!" Yet how many of them had any knowledge of the fact that Jesus was himself a Jew?

Amy-Jill Levine, Professor of New Testament and Jewish Studies at Vanderbilt Divinity School, writes, " . . . it is necessary to see Jesus as firmly within Judaism rather than standing apart from it, and it is essential that Judaism not be distorted through the filter of centuries of Christian stereotypes; a distorted picture of first-century Judaism inevitably leads to a distorted picture of Jesus. Just as bad: if we get Judaism wrong, we'll wind up perpetuating anti-Jewish or anti-Semitic teaching, and thus the mission of the church—to spread a gospel of love rather than a gospel of hate—will be undermined."[3]

While some people state that all four gospels make it clear that Jews killed Jesus, they miss the central meaning of what occurred.

3. Levine, *The Misunderstood Jew*, 7.

Jesus was himself a Jew who was killed by Roman power. Jews did not have the power to kill anyone, and crucifixion was not a Jewish instrument of death. It was, however, a commonly used Roman instrument of death. This is where historians disagree almost universally with biblical accounts.

Yes, I worship a crucified and risen Jew, as has every Christian throughout history. Let us join hands with our Jewish sisters and brothers for this and countless other reasons to stop the rise of anti-Semitic hate crimes today. What one act might you take today?

Jesus said to him, "I am the way, the truth, and the life. No one comes to the Father except through me."

JOHN 14:6

In 1948, Emmanuel Bronner, a master soap maker and German Jew, founded Dr. Bronner's Soap, which is Certified Fair Trade. He uses his labels to share the messages that, "We must realize our transcendent unity across religious and ethnic divides or perish" and "We are All-one or None!" The words ALL-ONE! are imprinted on each bar of soap, spreading his message of God's love for all people.

Jesus' words, "No one comes to the Father except through me," have been misused for centuries to proclaim the opposite message—one that says, "We are not all one unless everyone is Christian and believes Jesus is the long-awaited Messiah. Only Christians will be with their Creator in the after-life."

This is Fake News that has resulted in millions of deaths of non-Christians, particularly of Jews, religious-based hate crimes against people of many faiths, and more. So, if this is not what Jesus meant, what did he mean?

His words can be interpreted as rabbi-speak for, "See what I am doing? Do that." In other words, "Live as I have taught you to live. Love your neighbor as yourself. Welcome the stranger. Feed the hungry. Clothe the naked. Visit the prisoner. Then you will be with your Creator, not just in the after-life but in this life." What a different message this is!

Jesus does not say, "Unless you believe I am the Messiah, you will not see God, my Father." What he says is, "You cannot come to God except *through* me—through the way I have lived my life, through my example, through my teaching."

In 1989 the World Council of Churches issued this statement, "We cannot point to any other way of salvation than Jesus Christ; at the same time, we cannot set limits to the saving power of God." What a difference this understanding could make in our world.

Is there someone with whom you are called to share this True News?

*Meanwhile Saul, still breathing threats and murder against the disciples
of the LORD, went to the high priest and asked him for letters to the
synagogues at Damascus, so that if he found any that belonged to the
Way, men or women, he might bring them bound to Jerusalem. Now as
he was going along and approaching Damascus, suddenly a light from
heaven flashed around him. He fell to the ground and heard a voice
saying to him, "Saul, Saul, why do you persecute me?" He asked, "Where
are you, LORD?" The reply came, "I am Jesus who you are persecuting."*

ACTS 9:1–6

"Violence comes in many different forms, but hate has the same
DNA wherever you see it: whether in the form of ISIS, white su-
premacy, or genocide, it is the belief that another group is an ex-
istential threat to you and your community that often justifies the
most unspeakable acts of violence," stated Abbas Barzegar, Director
of Advocacy for the Council on American-Islamic Relations.[4]

During a six-week period in the Spring of 2019, there were
mass killings at a synagogue, churches, and mosques. The anti-
Semitic attack occurred outside San Diego at a celebration at the
end of Passover. Days earlier, Christians in Sri Lanka had been
massacred on Easter Sunday, while the previous month a man had
opened fire on two mosques in Christchurch, New Zealand.

The Summer of 2019 was similarly tragic with devestating
domestic terrorist attacks in back-to-back mass shootings. One in
El Paso, Texas on the morning of August 3rd targeted Hispanics
and killed twenty-two persons; the other was thirteen hours later in
Dayton, Ohio and killed nine.

Faced with such tragedy, the attacked often repeat one plaintive refrain, "We are good people, kind people. What did we ever
do to deserve this?"

I can only imagine that the early followers of Jesus who were
killed by Saul felt the same way. Then one day Saul, later known as
St. Paul, heard the voice of Jesus saying to him, "Saul, Saul, why do
you persecute me?"

4. Andone, "In the past 6 weeks," para. 31.

Could Jesus be saying these same words to us today through the words of those who are victimized? "Why are we persecuted?" Or, "why are you persecuting the One who created us?"

And that is the question, isn't it? Why are we persecuting our Creator? Why are those of us on the sidelines allowing the hate to spread?

What one thing might you do to help bring about positive change?

There is no longer Jew or Greek, there is no longer slave or free, there is no longer male and female; for all of you are one in Christ Jesus.

GALATIANS 3:28

Paul states succinctly in this verse that all people are equal in the eyes of God. Jew and Greek (or gentile), slave and free, male and female, we are all one in Christ Jesus. Any statement of inequality is Fake News in terms of what Scripture really says. As parts of the body of Christ, Christians believe all are equal yet distinctly different—all vitally needed for the good of the whole.

The rise of anti-Semitic hate crimes throughout the world belies this clear statement of Scripture. "Hate crime incidents targeting Jews and Jewish institutions in the U.S. spiked about 37 percent between 2016 and 2017, according to data released Tuesday by the FBI . . . It was the third year in a row hate offenses rose in the U.S . . . Hate crimes based on race, ethnicity or ancestry were the most common, making up about 60 percent of the total. Religious-based hate crime comprised about 20 percent of the total. The FBI data shows that Jewish people and institutions were most frequently targeted, accounting for 58 percent of religious-based hate crime incidents. Muslims were the second most frequent target, at 18.6 percent."[5]

In *The Diary of a Young Girl*, Anne Frank wrote, "It's always the same old story. No one wants to see the danger until it's staring them in the face."[6] The signs are clear. The signs are here. When will we see the danger that is all around us right now, today?

Paul's words in the Epistle to the Galatians were written over 2,000 years ago, yet, in terms of each oppressed group mentioned—Jews, slaves, and females—the discrimination continues and is increasing. Each one of us has a responsibility to share the True News of what Scripture says. We cannot keep silent in the face of the pure hatred that leads to mass killings of innocent people. For spiritual truth to belong to us and our neighbors, we must navigate our way through the darkness of hate and come into the light.

---

5. Donaghue, "New FBI data," para. 1, 2, 3.
6. Frank, *Diary,* 183.

In his book, *The Dignity of Difference*, Emeritus Chief Rabbi Jonathan Sacks writes, "The greatest single antidote to violence is *conversation*, speaking our fears, listening to the fears of others, and in that sharing of vulnerabilities discovering a genesis of hope."[7]

Is there someone with whom you might be called to begin a conversation?

7. Sacks, *Dignity of Difference*, 2.

Xenophobia

"When Mexico sends its people, they're not sending their best. They're sending people that have a lot of problems, and they're bringing those problems with us [*sic*]. They're bringing drugs. They're bringing crime. They're rapists. And some, I assume, are good people."[1]

Donald J. Trump, 2015

"Send her back! Send her back!"[2]

Supporters at 2019 Trump Rally referring to U.S. Representative Ilhan Omar

1. Mark, "Trump just referred," para. 2–3.
2. The New York Times, "Real Meaning," para. 2.

You know the heart of a stranger, for you were strangers in the land of Egypt.

EXODUS 23:9 (RSV)

At different times in our lives, we are all the stranger, standing at the threshold hoping for a word of welcome. As children, when we enter kindergarten, we are indeed the stranger to new surroundings and new expectations. Later as adults, we often find ourselves in the role of the stranger—in college, in the workplace, in new communities. Being the stranger is fundamental to the human experience. Simply being, living, moving through the life cycle, we will at times find ourselves strangers in an alien land, confused, seeking, and hoping for a warm welcome.

This is how we find ourselves in the story of God's people, for our Hebrew mothers and fathers were indeed strangers in an alien land. Their physical journey from bondage in Egypt through the wilderness toward the Promised Land parallels our own life journey with its many twists and turns, taking us to lands unknown, both physical and spiritual.[3]

There is a life-altering debate in America right now regarding immigration—whom to open our doors to and whom to keep at arm's length. Which religious minorities to let in and which to keep out. Whether to build a wall or not to build a wall. To separate children from their parents or to keep them together. To provide a toothbrush and soap or not to provide a toothbrush and soap!

Cradled within these discussions lies xenophobia, a fear of that which is foreign or strange. This fear of the "other" often lies at the heart of racism, sexism, heterosexism, anti-Semitism, anti-Muslim rhetoric, and more.

Chants by thousands of Americans at a July 2019 North Carolina Trump Rally of "Send her back! Send her back," in reference to Somali-born Representative Ilhan Omar, represents the height of fear of the other. It is a fear many of us never thought to see expressed by thousands of chanting Americans in the twenty-first century.

---

3. Geitz, *Fireweed Evangelism*, 85.

In the Civil Rights era, similar words were used to taunt African Americans who longed for equal education. People of faith, regardless of political persuasion, cannot look the other way when this happens. This depth of hatred for those who are different from us must stop, and it must stop immediately.

How different the response might be if we could connect with our own experience of being the "other," the stranger. It is not us versus them; it is all humankind together, struggling to find the common good. It is the most damaging kind of Fake News that makes us believe that some people are more worthy than others, that some have the right to label and belittle others, and that some have the right to stoke hatred and fear. Events in our country might look very different viewed through the lens of this Exodus passage.

Can you remember a time when you were the stranger? How did you feel?

*The LORD your God is God of gods and Lord of lords, the great God,
mighty and awesome, who is not partial and takes no bribe, who
executes justice for the orphan and the widow, and who loves the
strangers, providing them with food and clothing.*

DEUTERONOMY 10:17–18

One summer while on sabbatical, I embarked on a pilgrimage to
the Good Shepherd Home for Children in Cameroon, West Africa.
It was my first journey to a developing nation. Most of the one
hundred fifty children there were orphaned by the AIDS pandemic.
With 300,000 AIDS orphans in Cameroon and not one government
program to care for them, Anglican nun Sister Jane Mankaa has
dedicated her life to establishing two orphanages for the children to
see that justice prevails in their young, vulnerable lives.

While there, I spoke with many of the children and heard first-
hand their stories of heartbreak, abandonment, and abusive conditions in the extended families who initially took them in. Sister Jane
changed all of that.[4] They are no longer strangers, outcasts within
their extended families and villages. They are a loving family of one
hundred fifty sisters and brothers with one beloved mother, Sister
Jane. After meeting with several of the children, they are no longer strangers to me. I was deeply moved, and the following poem
poured out of me:

Empty Hearts

Has anyone tried to count the tears
Of AIDS orphans left behind?
Worn out photographs of happier times
Gazed upon in silent moments of empty grief?
Empty of a mother's arms
Empty of a father's smile
Resulting in empty stomachs,
Empty wallets,
Empty hearts.

4. Geitz, *I Am That Child*, 41–44, 56–60, 71–73, 89–91, 118–120, 146–148,
159–163.

Has anyone tried to count the tears
Of AIDS orphans left behind?
Would anyone dare?
Elizabeth Geitz

Have you ever visited a developing nation? If so, what was that like for you? If not, could you perhaps study life in a part of the world culturally different from your own? Could your Creator be calling you to reach out to "the stranger" in other countries?

This is the LORD's doing. It is marvelous in our eyes.

PSALM 118:23

There are times when we may feel drawn to work with and for people we have never met, who are strangers in every sense of the word—literal strangers, cultural strangers, ethnic strangers, and more. Saying "yes" to such a pull can feel like jumping off the high dive for the first time, catapulting us into the unknown, leaving us feeling both exhilarated and afraid.

Such was my experience joining in partnership with my Cameroonian neighbor, Sister Jane Mankaa. Several years after visiting the orphanage she founded in Cameroon, she asked me to join her in a cross-cultural partnership to build a residential secondary/high school for 350 Cameroonian students.

My first response was, "I can't possibly help you. I know nothing about construction, much less about building a school 5,000 miles from home!" But as time went on, I gradually realized that, yes, I could partner with my sister. Yes, together our gifts and skills could change the lives of Cameroonian children for generations to come.

Six years later, Sister Jane and I both marvel at what has occurred. After prayer and painstakingly hard work, we rejoice in "the Lord's doing." Over five hundred people have joined the journey with us. The first two phases of construction were completed on time and within budget, and Good Shepherd Academy in Bafut, Cameroon was born.[5]

Joining hands with our neighbors in developing countries can yield rich rewards, taking us out of ourselves and our privileged lives in the first world and into deep bonds of sisterhood and brotherhood across borders and thousands of miles. We may often feel that there is little we can do to truly have an impact or make a difference in today's world. But this is Fake News! We can make a difference, each one of us, if only we take the first step and move out of our comfort zone into the unknown; if only we are willing to

5. See ImaginingTomorrow.org.

embrace the strangers we have never met and to dedicate our lives to learning about and from them.

As American anthropologist Margaret Mead is said to have written, "Never doubt that a small group of thoughtful, committed, citizens can change the world. Indeed, it is the only thing that ever has."

Might the Divine Feminine be calling you to join hands with a neighbor in a developing country? How might you reach out?

How long, O LORD? Will you forget me forever? How long will you
hide your face from me?

PSALM 13:1

Mass shootings in the United States have reached epidemic proportions. As of October 28, 2019, there have been 2,271 gun massacres since the Sandy Hook Elementary School mass shooting in 2012.[6] In many cases, the root cause is xenophobia, the fear or hatred of those who are perceived to be "other" or foreign. The El Paso Walmart gun massacre resulted from hatred of Hispanics; the Pulse nightclub shooting from hatred of gays; the Charleston church massacre from hatred of African Americans. Fake News about each of these groups led to the deaths of countless innocent people.

As a spirituality columnist, I penned the words below following the shock of Sandy Hook. I was filled with both anger and a deep longing for change when I wrote them. Seven years later, nothing has changed. I am still angry. I still long. I share these words with you here with prayers for a better tomorrow.

Right now at this very moment, I am being held hostage. As are you and every citizen of this great land we are privileged to call home. I am being held hostage by the NRA. At gunpoint. Right now.

I cannot walk into any shopping mall, movie theater, university, or even kindergarten classroom without knowing somewhere buried in the deep recesses of my mind that I could be shot at a moment's notice. Knowing that my loved ones could be gunned down as they unsuspectingly shop, watch a movie, study, or teach in school.

What is wrong with our country that we allow one powerful lobby to win time and again to allow weapons of war to be sold legally in the United States? And for what? The second amendment right to bear arms? There were no such weapons when that amendment was written and everyone with a fifth-grade education knows that, unless they were gunned down in their classroom before making it to fifth grade.

6. Vox.com, "After Sandy Hook," para. 1.

Because assault-style weapons are needed for game hunting? Like most Southerners, I grew up in a family of hunters. My dad and two brothers loved the camaraderie of duck hunting every fall, as did my husband and his father with deer and pheasant. They were and are special parent/child times.

I used to hunt deer. The only deer I ever pulled a trigger to shoot was killed with one bullet from a distance of one hundred fifty yards. There is simply no reason to have an assault-style weapon to be a sporting gun enthusiast. Absolutely no reason to have one at all, other than to kill large numbers of innocent people in a short period of time.

As a sporting clay enthusiast today, I do not need to go into a gun show and buy a gun without a background check. And I do not need to be on a clays course with anyone who has been able to do so. Such laws are as detrimental to serious hunters or clay shooters as they are to the general population.

I am being held hostage by the NRA. And so are you.

The belief that assault-style weapons do not greatly increase the number of people who can be murdered quickly is deadly Fake News that kills innocent children.

How long, O Lord, how long?

I was hungry and you gave me food, I was thirsty and you gave me something to drink, I was a stranger and you welcomed me . . . When you did it to one of the least of these who are members of my family, you did it to me.

MATTHEW 25:35–36

A former microfinance officer named Neh is one of the more than 437,000 English-speaking Cameroonians displaced as a result of armed conflict between Anglophone Cameroonians and the Francophone government.[7] What began as a peaceful protest against marginalization and language issues in education and law continued with mass arrests and government soldiers in helicopters allegedly killing civilians who were protesting, according to eyewitnesses and rights groups.[8]

I was in Bamenda, Cameroon in November 2016, when I happened upon the first demonstration by educators and hundreds of lawyers wearing black robes and white wigs. Suddenly several loud "pops" rang out, which turned out to be tear gas launched by government gendarmes. The peaceful, orderly march was over.

Three years later 3,000 people have been killed, entire Anglophone villages burned, and businesses and crops destroyed. As a result, English-speaking Cameroonians have fled for their lives—some to neighboring Nigeria and some finding their way to the U.S./Mexico border with dreams of living in safety.

"It is just too much," sobbed Neh, who stated that she had been arrested, beaten, and raped by soldiers in Cameroon. Speaking to a reporter from *The Guardian* at a protest camp in Mexico set up by African migrants she shared further, "We thought our suffering was almost over. And now we're stuck here, treated like the lowest citizens on earth."[9]

With the number of refugees allowed into the United States currently capped at 18,000/year, a record low, thousands of people like Neh are caught in the middle with nowhere to go.

7. Baloch, "UNHCR says funds," para. 4.
8. McAllister, "Cameroon army helicopters," para. 1, 6–8.
9. Tuckman, "We've been taken," para. 3–4.

Are decreased entry numbers due to a lack of available physical space? No. Reports to the contrary are Fake News meant to mislead Americans into believing that there is no room for the stranger. Concrete examples belie this belief.

Take Clarkston, Georgia for instance. "As many white residents fled farther out to more fashionable developing Atlanta suburbs, Clarkston became perfect for refugees, with its hundreds of vacated apartments and access to public transportation, a post office, and a grocery store, all within walking distance."[10]

Similarly, in Rust Belt cities like Buffalo, New York, immigrants have reinvigorated the economy. Now "medical clinics have closed down, housing developments have stalled, and employers have been left looking for employees . . . The loss for refugees hoping to come to America appears to also be a loss for the communities they might have called home."[11]

Jesus tells us in Matthew 25 that, when we welcome the stranger, we welcome none other than Jesus himself. Likewise, when we turn the stranger away, or worse, abuse him or her in any way, it is Jesus whom we are abusing.

Can you hear the cries of Neh and the people in her situation? What might we learn from the hospitality of cities like Clarkson and Buffalo, who have welcomed countless refugees with warm hearts and open arms?

10. Misra, "Cities," para. 11.
11. Misra, "Cities," para. 15.

*Do not neglect to show hospitality to strangers, for by doing that some
have entertained angels without knowing it.*

HEBREWS 13:2

When we are called to show hospitality to strangers, we are called to
be hosts in the truest sense of the word. It is awareness of the Divine
presence within such relationships that enables us to be not only
hosts but guests. For this to occur when we engage in dialogue with
the stranger, we need to participate in mutual listening. We must be
willing not only to give in the name of God but to receive as well,
for what often comes to us in and through the other's utterances is
nothing less than God's word for us.

This guest/host reversal is vividly depicted in the story of
Abraham welcoming three heavenly strangers in Genesis 18:1–15.
Abraham runs from his tent to meet them, bows, and then offers
them water, rest, and food. As they are eating the meal prepared for
them, one of the strangers reveals God's word to Sarah and Abraham. Sarah is to have a son in her old age. In reflecting on this passage from Genesis, the author of the Letter to the Hebrews wrote:
"Let mutual love continue. Do not neglect to show hospitality to
strangers, for by doing that some have entertained angels without
knowing it" (Heb. 13:1–2). Just as these angels were messengers to
Sarah and Abraham, the angels our Creator sends to us today are
heavenly messengers to us.

A similar guest/host reversal is found in Luke's gospel following the crucifixion of Jesus, when two people on the road to Emmaus
encounter a stranger. They act as host to him, telling their story of
the death of Jesus, then listen as the stranger shares his knowledge
of Scripture (Luke 24:13–27). As they come to the village to which
they are going, the stranger walks ahead as if he is going on. "But
they urged him strongly, saying, 'Stay with us, because it is almost
evening and the day is now nearly over'" (Luke 24:29). It is through
this act of inviting the stranger to stay with them and break bread
that they learn it is Jesus to whom they are speaking. The hosts to
the stranger become the guests of Christ. As guests, they hear God's

word for them. If they had never reached out to this stranger, how different their lives would have been.[12]

Hospitality to the stranger was a hallmark of the kingdom of God in Scripture, just as it is today. Is someone waiting for you to reach out and welcome them? Who might it be?

12. Geitz, *Fireweed Evangelism*, 92–93.

Let every person be subject to the governing authorities; for there is no authority except from God, and those authorities that exist have been instituted by God. Therefore whoever resists authority resists what God has appointed, and those who resist will incur judgment.

ROMANS 13:1–2

In former Attorney General Jeff Session's address to law enforcement officers in June 2018, he cited Romans 13 to explain why he had launched a zero-tolerance policy of separating families who were seeking illegal entry into the United States. At that time two thousand children had been separated from their parents in an attempt to stop illegal border crossings.

"I would cite you to the Apostle Paul and his clear and wise command in Romans 13, to obey the laws of government because God has ordained them for the purpose of order," Sessions said.[13] Citing Scripture to justify separating children from their parents is a horrifying example of Fake News being used to tear peoples' hearts and lives apart.

And it is not new. Romans 13 has been invoked in similar situations throughout history. "British Royals cited it to chastise rebellious American revolutionaries. Slave owners in early America justified the institution of slavery by quoting it. American law authorized slave owners to separate black sons and daughters from mothers and fathers by selling them to another slave owner . . . The Nazis in Germany and apartheid South Africa quoted Romans 13 to give religious authority to genocide and apartheid."[14]

The abuse of Scripture to uphold a white patriarchal system is nothing new. Yet one would hope that history alone would have given Attorney General Sessions pause to reconsider citing this passage in the year 2018.

Every word of the New Testament has one standard of authenticity and one only. Is it in accordance with the teachings of Jesus? Throughout his life, Jesus stood for the way of love, the way of compassion, of loving our neighbor as ourselves. Pulling one verse out of context to be used for a purpose antithetical to Jesus' teaching is

13. Gonzales, "Sessions Cites," para. 2.
14. Jackson, "Slave owners," para. 4, 6.

called heresy in religious circles, as Sessions soon discovered when he was publicly chastised and threatened with expulsion by over six hundred pastors and members of his own denomination, The United Methodist Church.

When will such abuse of Scripture stop? What one step might you take to call it out when you see it?

You shall not kill.

Exodus 20:13

The Ten Commandments contain some of the most well-known ethical principles in the Bible. Even so, the fifth commandment, "You shall not kill," is so undervalued in America that so far there have been more mass shootings than days in 2019.[15]

Back-to-back gun massacres on August 3, 2019 in El Paso and Dayton have rocked Americans to their core. Once again, we see shocked, weeping survivors and family members who will never again see their loved ones. Once again, we ask how this could happen. Once again, we are stunned at the inhumanity of it all.

It is well documented that the 2019 El Paso massacre targeted Hispanics and killed twenty-two people; that the 2018 Pittsburgh synagogue shooting targeted Jews and killed eleven; that the 2016 Orlando nightclub massacre targeted gays and killed forty-nine; that the 2015 Charleston church shooting targeted African Americans and killed nine.

It is also well documented that 94 percent of Americans support background checks for all gun buyers.[16] It is past time to effect the changes needed to bring our laws in line with the will of the people.

What isn't as well known is that a common trait among mass killers is their hatred toward women. This is where sexism, racism, heterosexism, anti-Semitism, and xenophobia trip over each other in a macabre death spiral. "The fact that mass shootings are almost exclusively perpetrated by men is 'missing from the national conversation,' said Governor Gavin Newsome of California."[17]

While the motivations of men who commit mass murder are complex, there is one common thread other than access to firearms—"a history of hating women, assaulting wives, girlfriends and female family members, or sharing misogynistic views online."[18]

---

15. Silverstein, "There have been," para. 1.
16. Montanaro, "Americans Largely Support," para. 15.
17. Bosman et al., "A Common Trait," para. 4.
18. Bosman et al., "A Common Trait," para. 4.

The man who was convicted of killing twenty-six people in a Texas church in 2017 was a perpetrator of domestic violence who threatened to kill his wife. The mass murderer of forty-nine people at the Pulse nightclub in Orlando beat his pregnant wife. The Dayton shooter who killed eleven had a history of threatening violence against female classmates.

Hate begets hate, and the common denominator is hatred of women. The patriarchal system in which we all live has led not only to discrimination against women, but discrimination and hatred of the other, whether the other is gay, black, brown, Jew, Christian, or Muslim. We are all "the other" to someone. Let that sink in for a moment.

God created humankind in God's image; in the image of God, God created them; male and female he created them. God saw everything he had made and, indeed, it was very good.

Let's start there. Shall we?

Women Leaders

"The feminist agenda is not about equal rights for women.
It is about a socialist, anti-family, political movement that
encourages women to leave their husbands, kill their children,
practice witchcraft, destroy capitalism, and become lesbians."[1]

Pat Robertson

"I don't know if our country is ready for a female president."[2]

Dawn Zimmerman

1. Associated Press, "Robertson Letter," A16.
2. Feldman, "Most American Women," para. 4.

The king of Egypt said to the Hebrew midwives, one of whom was named Shiphrah and the other Puah, "When you act as midwives to the Hebrew women, and see them on the birth stool, if it is a boy, kill him; but if it is a girl, she shall live." But the midwives feared God; they did not do as the king of Egypt commanded them, but they let the boys live.

EXODUS 1:15–17

"I don't know if America is ready for a female president." How many times have I heard this refrain? And the origin of such strongly held belief? The Bible. After centuries of biblical interpretation promoting a patriarchal agenda, women and men alike believe that God created woman as inferior to man, that women are not natural-born leaders.

This Fake News regarding half of humankind is easily disproven with a careful reading of Scripture. Let us walk through the Bible together and learn of the many powerful female leaders within it—women who have defied kings, led armies, participated in salvation history, saved entire peoples, ruled nations, and more. Let's begin with two midwives in ancient Egypt.

Imagine the anxiety Shiphrah and Puah feel when their king summons them. They are enslaved midwives who are singled out and ordered to kill all male Hebrew babies. Their purpose in life is to preserve the life of mother and child, yet suddenly they are commanded to become murderers.

There is no hint in this story of a struggle with their conscience about whom to obey. Shiphrah and Puah immediately know what to do. Courageously risking their own lives, they defy the Egyptian king's orders and save the lives of countless male Hebrew babies. Why? Because they know the king's command is contrary to the laws of their Divine Mother. When the king asks why they have allowed the boys to live, they shrewdly deceive him, and "so God dealt well with the midwives."

Not only are Shiphrah and Puah brave, they are also perceptive and inventive. When asked a direct question by the king that would have implicated them in a plot to disobey his orders, they know exactly how to respond to save both themselves and the male infants yet to be born.

What inner strength it must have taken for these two women to act so boldly in defiance of their king. Fearlessly challenging unjust structures was a hallmark of the Hebrew prophets and the life and ministry of Jesus.

Could Shiphrah and Puah have been role models for Jesus? Could they be role models for you?

Then Moses' sister Miriam said to Pharaoh's daughter, "Shall I go and get you a nurse from the Hebrew women to nurse the child for you?"

EXODUS 2:7

There are times when our voices can change the course of history. That time is now. The students of Stoneman Douglas High School in Parkland, Florida who survived a 2018 mass school shooting are using their voices to begin and continue a grassroots movement to change U.S. gun laws. Their intent is to save innocent lives, much as Moses' sister Miriam does at another time in history when innocent children are also being killed.

When Moses is born, the Hebrews have been in Israel for generations and are becoming so great in number that the Pharaoh fears they will someday rise against him. As a result, he decrees that all male Hebrew babies are to be killed.

To save his life, Moses' mother hides him for three months. If she had not been brave enough to do so, Moses would have been murdered along with the other male Hebrew babies. Most certainly, his mother's own life would have been in danger if her secret had been discovered. Yet she risks her life, unknowingly setting in motion the liberation of the Hebrew people.

After three months, Moses' mother places her infant son in a papyrus basket in the river as his sister Miriam watches from a distance. While the king's daughter is bathing in the river, she sees the baby and rescues him. Although she is an enslaved person, Miriam immediately addresses the princess and offers to find a Hebrew woman to nurse the baby. Who does this resourceful girl choose? Moses' own mother. Though only a child, Miriam also saves Moses' life, forever changing the course of spiritual history.

Have you ever taken a risk and spoken out when others were afraid to do so? How did it feel? If not, what changes might you make to be more like Miriam and the Stoneman Douglas students?

The prophet Miriam, Aaron's sister, took a tambourine in her hand; and all the women went out after her with tambourines and with dancing.

EXODUS 15:20

Hear what the LORD says . . . "I sent before you Moses, Aaron, and Miriam."

MICAH 6:1, 4

Enslaved in Egypt for approximately four hundred years, the Israelites tirelessly beseech God to hear their prayers and deliver them from the hands of their enemies. In answer to their prayers, God lifts up not one leader, as often depicted, but three.

The belief that Moses alone led the Israelites out of bondage in Egypt toward the Promised Land is more Fake News. Moses' sister and brother, Miriam and Aaron, are also sent to lead the exodus journey. All three of them are identified as leaders, yet only Moses is remembered as such.

Has someone else ever gotten all the recognition for something in which you played a significant role? This is what happened to Miriam and Aaron; history has forgotten them.

Not only does Miriam help save Moses' life when he's an infant and assist him in leading the exodus, but she is also designated in Scripture as a prophet, indicating that her community holds her in high esteem. Lifesaver, leader, and prophet—Miriam was indeed a remarkable and versatile young woman.

Miriam is also wise enough to celebrate their exodus victory by leading the women in dancing and the shaking of tambourines; the women all follow her. She was clearly in a leadership role on the long and arduous journey. I have no doubt she listened to many a story and dried many a tear along the way, comforting and cajoling at just the right time. Then, when danger is past, Miriam knows how to have fun and celebrate a victory, something we often gloss over in our busy lives.

Numerous women were in leadership roles over three thousand years ago. How might you share this True News with others?

*Then the daughters of Zelophehad came forward. The names of
his daughters were: Mahlah, Noah, Noglah, Milcah, and Tirzah.
They stood before Moses, Eleazar the priest, the leaders, and all the
congregation, at the entrance of the tent of meeting, and they said . . .
"Give to us a possession among our father's brothers." Moses brought
their case before the LORD. And the LORD spoke to Moses, saying: "The
daughters of Zelophehad are right in what they are saying; you shall
indeed let them possess an inheritance among their father's brothers
and pass the inheritance of their father on to them."*

NUMBERS 27:1–7

When the Taliban gained control of the Swat Valley of Pakistan in
2007, human rights violations and killings were rampant. One brave
girl dared to tell the story of young girls and women living under
this brutal regime by writing for the BBC in Urdu under the pen
name of Gul Maka. That girl was Malala Yousafzai. Returning from
class on a school bus in 2012, she was shot in the head by the Taliban
at point-blank range. She was fifteen years old. Her crime? Speaking
out publicly for the right of Pakistani girls to receive an education.[3]

When Zelophehad dies without a male heir in 1260 BCE, his
daughters present a convincing case before Moses to keep their father's name and inherit his property. In their culture, their actions
are bold indeed and exhibit great strength and courage. Contrary
to the laws of the day, the Lord confirms the women's position.
This simple act speaks volumes to me about our Creator's view of
women and their rights.

Malala not only survived the shooting, but she also went on to
campaign for girl's education on an international stage and in 2014
was awarded the Nobel Peace Prize. She is the youngest recipient in
history. Many referred to her recovery as miraculous, and so it was.
I believe that, once again, God intervened in history to uphold the
rights of women. God has spoken.

Today, more and more women are speaking out when their
rights are violated. Here's to Zelophehad's daughters and Malala for
paving the way!

3. Yousafzai with Lamb, *I Am Malala.*

Then she [Rahab] said [to the king's men], "True, the men came to me, but I did not know where they came from. And when it was time to close the gate at dark, the men went out. Where the men went I do not know. Pursue them quickly, for you can overtake them."

JOSHUA 2:4-5

Another unsung female hero in the Bible is a prostitute named Rahab, who willingly risks her life to save the Hebrew people. When Moses dies, Joshua is chosen to lead the Israelites into the Promised Land. Since they must overtake the city of Jericho to reach their destination, Joshua sends ahead two spies as scouts.

They come to the home of Rahab, who cunningly hides them on her roof under stalks of flax. The king suspects the spies' presence and has his men question Rahab, who risks her life by deceiving the king and sending his army in the wrong direction. When all is safe, Rahab declares her belief in Joshua's God, then asks for mercy for her family when her city is overtaken.

Rahab's first thoughts in time of danger are not of herself, but of her family. Not only does her courage and ingenuity save her own family, but she saves the Israelite people as well.

Both Jewish and Christian faiths have long held that Moses and then Joshua, alone with God's help, were responsible for getting the Israelites to the Promised Land. Yet, this is more Fake News! Miriam and Aaron, Moses' sister and brother, also helped lead the exodus and Rahab's aid to their journey was life-saving. Without Miriam and Rahab, the outcome would have been significantly different.

It is past time to recover this part of biblical history. It is past time for women to receive the recognition they deserve. It is past time to accept that women can be and always have been leaders.

What woman might you champion today?

*At that time Deborah, a prophetess, wife of Lappidoth, was judging
Israel. She used to sit under the palm of Deborah . . . and the Israelites
came up to her for judgment.*

JUDGES 4:4–5

On June 11, 1970, Colonel Anna Mae Hays, Chief of the Army
Nurse Corps, was promoted to the grade of Brigadier General. She
became the first woman in the history of the United States Army to
wear the insignia of a brigadier general.[4]

She received thousands of pieces of correspondence acknowl-
edging her promotion, some of which were quite amusing. For
example, a letter from Germany was addressed to "Mrs. Brigade
General Anna Mae Hays, Chief of the Feminine Army Sanitary
Corps. On one occasion, General William Westmoreland's wife,
Kitsy, remarked to Hays, 'I wish you would get married again.'
When Hays inquired why, Westmoreland responded, 'I want some
man to learn what it's like to be married to a general.'"[5]

Today there are seven female generals in the United States, an
accomplishment that is heralded as groundbreaking, a new phe-
nomenon in military history. But female military leaders are as old
as the Bible itself.

Deborah skillfully commanded military troops and is also
the only female judge in Scripture. When she believes the Divine
Feminine is calling her to send troops into battle, she does so without hesitation—all ten thousand of them. She summons Barak, a
general, who states, "If you will go with me, I will go; but if you
will not go with me, I will not go." Imagine a general making such
a request in the patriarchal society in which the Bible was written,
when women were considered the property of men. Deborah goes
as requested and the troops are victorious.

There is no doubt that Deborah had a clear sense of her own
authority and was comfortable in a leadership role over three
thousand years ago. Women have been in strong, visible positions
of leadership for thousands of years, yet women today are still

4. Sarnecky, "Brigadier General Anna Mae Hays," para. 3.
5. Sarnecky, "Brigadier General Anna Mae Hays," para. 4.

under-represented in top leadership positions both in the United States and around the world.

Is there a woman leader you might affirm today?

David said to Abigail, "Blessed be the LORD, the God of Israel, who sent you to meet me today! Blessed be your good sense, and blessed be you, who have kept me today from bloodguilt and from avenging myself by my own hand . . . Then David . . . said to her, "Go up to your house in peace; see. I have heeded your voice, and I have granted your petition."

1 SAMUEL 25:32–35

During a potential life and death conflict, Abigail's wit and initiative save the life of her husband Nabal and his men, as well as the lives of everyone in the enemy camp. How did it all start?

David protected Nabal's shepherds, so David asks for a gift in return. Being "so ill-natured no one can speak to him," Nabal refuses. In response, David prepares his men for battle. Abigail learns of the impending battle and acts quickly and decisively. Without her husband's knowledge, she has her donkeys laden with food and then rides off to meet his adversary on a mission of peace. Abigail uses her skills of persuasion and convinces David to accept the food and stop the attack. While David's immediate response to Nabal's refusal is, "Every man strap on his sword!" Abigail's response is to undertake a mission of peace.

Women are often the peacemakers in today's world. In 2017, a group of Palestinian and Israeli women known as Women Wage for Peace dressed in white and marched for two weeks through the desert, ending in a meeting in a tent of reconciliation. We are "from the right, the left, Jews and Arabs, from the cities and the periphery and we have decided that we will stop the next war," said Marilyn Smadja, one of the founders of the group.[6]

What a role model Abigail can be for them. What a role model she can be for all of us who long for peace wherever we live. Do you ever find yourself in the role of peacemaker? How might Abigail be a role model for you?

---

6. Worley, "Thousands of Palestinian," para. 4.

When the queen of Sheba heard of the fame of Solomon . . . she came to test him with hard questions. She came to Jerusalem with a very great retinue, with camels bearing spices, and very much gold, and precious stones; and when she came to Solomon, she told him all that was on her mind.

1 KINGS 10:1–2

The Queen of Sheba is popularly known as a glamorous African queen who was involved in a romance with King Solomon. Portrayals of her throughout history and in films are of a stunning woman, well-coifed, and dripping with precious jewels. Yet this portrayal of her is, you guessed it, Fake News.

Sheba is a kingdom mentioned in the Hebrew Bible/Old Testament and in the Qur'an. While the Queen of Sheba remains unnamed, she is believed to have been Queen Makeda of Ethiopia.

The most recent movie version of her life stars Halle Berry in the lead role. This is a more accurate depiction of her than previously, for the Queen of Sheba was most likely Ethiopian and therefore black. However, it is still not an accurate portrayal.

According to biblical tradition, the Queen of Sheba's beauty is not part of her mystique. Rather, she is portrayed as a ruler of wisdom, wealth, and power. Her abundant self-assurance is obvious. She willingly travels a great distance to test King Solomon's wisdom with her own and to speak all that is on her mind.

The Queen of Sheba is a woman who knows how to travel. Leaving no stone unturned, she arrives with camels, spices, gold, and precious stones. She immediately makes it clear that she is Solomon's equal in every respect, testing him with hard questions and matching his knowledge with her own. When he surpasses her expectations, she offers him a rhetorically perfect speech, culminating in the praise of his God.

How often it is that only a woman's appearance is commented upon for better or worse, rather than her intellect or accomplishments. This misrepresentation of a woman's strengths is just as prevalent today as it was in biblical times, and it is past time for it to stop.

How might you best laud our sisters' strengths?

So the priest Hilkiah, Ahikam, Achbor, Shaphan, and Asaiah went to the prophetess Huldah the wife of Shallum . . . where they consulted her.

2 KINGS 22:14

"Act Now or We Will," "System Change, Not Climate Change," read the signs held by teen activists outside the U.N. on August 30, 2019. Sixteen-year-old Greta Thunberg had just sailed into New York Harbor on a zero-emission boat and was on hand to attend an impromptu meeting at the United Nations. The Swedish teen had crossed rough seas from the U.K. on a two-week journey to demand that government leaders heed the scientific warnings regarding the irreversible effects of climate change. Refusing to fly to the United States due to polluting emissions, Thunberg lives what she advocates.

In her challenge to the 2019 World Economic Forum in Davos, Switzerland, Thunberg stated emphatically, "Some people say that the climate crisis is something that we all have created. But that is just another convenient lie. Because if everyone is guilty then no one is to blame. And someone is to blame. Some people—some companies and some decision makers in particular— have known exactly what priceless values they are sacrificing to continue making unimaginable amounts of money.

I want to challenge those companies and those decision makers into real and bold climate action. To set their economic goals aside and to safeguard the future living conditions for humankind. I don't believe for one second that you will rise to the challenge. But I want to ask you all the same. I ask you to prove me wrong. For the sake of your children, for the sake of your grandchildren. For the sake of life and this beautiful living planet."[7]

These are the words of a prophet.

When Greta was mocked online for having Asperger's syndrome, she wrote back, "I have Asperger's syndrome and that means I'm sometimes a bit different from the norm. And—given the right circumstances—being different is a superpower."[8] Standing up for oneself and staying on message regardless of the circumstances is

7. Thunberg, "Our House is On Fire," para. 14–18.
8. Brazell, "Greta Thunberg," para. 9–10.

the mark of a true leader and prophet in the cruel world of social media bullying.

According to Jewish tradition, Huldah was one of seven women prophets in the Bible. Along with the prophet Jeremiah, she lived in Jerusalem during the reign of King Josiah in the year 627 BCE. According to the Jewish Midrash, Huldah led a school for women in Jerusalem, where she taught Scripture as it pertained to Jewish women, mothers, and daughters.

After the Book of the Law was discovered during renovations of Solomon's temple, the king commanded several men, including the priest Hilkiah, to inquire of the Lord concerning the words of the book. To whom did they turn? To Huldah, who interpreted the Scriptures for them.

Greta Thunberg, like Huldah, is a prophet in every sense of the word. Not all prophets are men. Not all prophets are adults. How might our world be different if we heeded the words of Greta Thunberg? Is there one change you could make in your life to help?

I am my beloved's, and his desire is for me. Come, my beloved, let us go forth into the fields, and lodge in the villages; let us go out early to the vineyards . . . There I will give you my love . . . If I met you outside, I would kiss you, and no one would despise me. I would lead you and bring you into the house of my mother, and into the chamber of the one who bore me. I would give you spiced wine to drink, the juice of my pomegranates. O that his left hand were under my head, and that his right hand embraced me!

SONG OF SOLOMON 7:10–13, 8:1–3

These passionate, lustful, romantic words are spoken in the Song of Solomon by the Shulamite Woman, who speaks more than any other woman in the Hebrew Bible/Old Testament and in the New Testament. "Hot, sensual, and evocative language holds sway here . . . Because of its evocative and sexual words spoken mostly by a woman, the authorship of the Song has been the subject of endless debates."[9] What cannot be debated, however, is the large amount of air time this woman is given in the Bible and how refreshing it is!

In the conservative Southern church in which I was raised, this passage was not taught. Female sexuality was rarely discussed, if ever, except within the prevalent discussions of "no sex outside marriage."

Women today, especially those who grew up in conservative religious traditions, need to reclaim their sensuality and their right to express it. They need to embrace their sexuality as the God-given gift it is. Just this week, I saw a "groundbreaking" video on social media of women discussing sex and pleasure. Groundbreaking. In 2019.

To deny that women are healthy sexual beings created in the image of God is nothing less than more Fake News meant to keep women in their place.

Does this passage change your view of Scripture? Or does it change your view of yourself and the people in your life?

---

9. Freeman, *Bible Women*, 293.

Then Esther said in reply to Mordecai, "Go, gather all the Jews to be found in Susa, and hold a fast on my behalf, and neither eat nor drink for three days, night or day. I and my maids will also fast as you do. After that I will go to the king, though it is against the law; and if I perish, I perish."

ESTHER 4:15-16

Queen Esther was married to the Persian King Ahasuerus, a divorced gentile. Without the king's knowledge, his chief courtier Haman ordered the execution of all Jews in the kingdom. The king doesn't know Esther is Jewish and she agonizes over whether to reveal her identity.

Esther prays to her Divine Mother to save her from her fear, and her prayers are answered. At great risk to herself, she decides to reveal her identity. She tells the king, "Let my life be granted me at my petition, and my people at my request. For we have been sold, I and my people, to be destroyed."

As a result of her willingness to be vulnerable, all Jews in the kingdom are saved. And Esther is not alone. She follows the example of a long line of Jewish women who risked their lives to save others—Miriam and her mother, who saved the infant Moses; the midwives Shiphrah and Puah, who saved numerous male Hebrew babies; Rahab, who saved Joshua's spies and, therefore, the people of Israel, and more.

Have you ever been afraid to reveal something about yourself for fear of the consequences? It took me years to speak publicly about my mother's suicide for fear of what others might think. Yet, when I finally did so, I experienced life-giving freedom.

Are you harboring anything that needs to be brought into the light and shared? Could Esther be a role model for you?

In those days Mary set out and went with haste to a Judean town in the hill country, where she entered the house of Zechariah and greeted Elizabeth . . . And Mary remained with her about three months and then returned to her home.

LUKE 1:39, 56

The Mary whom we meet in this passage is the woman who will become the mother of Jesus. As such she is later designated as *theotokos,* God-bearer, a title held by no other person in history. The greatness of this young woman who will endure the unthinkable—watching her son die an agonizing death—is yet to be revealed.

Here we see her as a teenager, faced with the most perplexing time of her life. What does she do? Mary knows she needs a girlfriend and she needs one immediately. Suddenly she remembers the old woman Elizabeth, unable to conceive for years, now pregnant with the child later known as John the Baptist. So, Mary leaves "with haste" and flees to the hill country. There's a lot of living and a lot of humanity revealed in those words.

Mary doesn't tell Joseph, her parents, or a close relative. She knows what she needs, a woman who can understand, so she leaves as quickly as possible. It is three months before Mary returns home.

In her book, *You Gotta Have Girlfriends,* Suzanne Braun Levine shows us that one of the best things any woman can do for her health is to nurture relationships with her girlfriends. She writes, "Not only do our girlfriends keep us physically healthy, but their support can also make us well when we are sick. A study of breast cancer patients by researchers at Ohio State University's Comprehensive Cancer Center found that those who were in a supervised support group were 56 percent less likely to die than those who were going it alone."[10] New studies even show that women can change one another's brain chemistry for the better.[11]

As Mary knew, those many years ago, our girlfriends can be a lifeline to us when we are sinking under the weight of unexpected

---

10. Levine, *You Gotta,* loc. 25.
11. Levine, *You Gotta,* loc. 25.

news. When did you last spend time alone with a girlfriend or a group of women friends? How did you feel?

Can you follow Mary's example and reach out?

Jesus said . . . "Truly I tell you, wherever the good news is proclaimed in the whole world, what she has done will be told in remembrance of her."

MARK 14:6, 9

While Jesus is dining in Bethany at the home of Simon, a woman breaks into the room carrying an alabaster jar. She then anoints Jesus' head with a costly ointment. As a result, she is scolded by several men at the dinner. Jesus replies, "Let her alone; why do you trouble her?"

Her anointing can be viewed as a prophetic recognition of Jesus as the Christ, since the Messiah would receive such an anointing. So significant is her action to Jesus that he wants her to be remembered wherever the gospel is proclaimed throughout the world. What an affirmation of her gift!

Even though her story is recounted in all four gospels, this intuitive woman's anointing of Jesus has indeed been forgotten. In her book, *In Memory of Her,* Elisabeth Schüssler Fiorenza writes, "Wherever the gospel is proclaimed and the eucharist celebrated another story is told: the story of the apostle who betrayed Jesus. The name of the betrayer is remembered, but the name of the faithful disciple is forgotten because she was a woman."[12]

Since many other memorable women throughout history have been forgotten, it is our duty to keep their stories alive. We need to proclaim the True News that the prophet Anna, Martha, Mary of Bethany, and the Samaritan woman at the well all recognized Jesus as the Messiah, each taking a courageous stand in the face of disbelievers.

How can we affirm women today who take courageous stands? Courtney Wild, an alleged child victim of convicted sex offender Jeffrey Epstein, was one of his first victims to reveal her identity. She then urged others who were also allegedly raped when underage to come forward. May her courage in the face of glaring publicity and the relentless questioning of her past also be remembered.

What woman do you need to uphold so that her story will be remembered for all time?

---

12. Fiorenza, *In Memory of Her,* xiii.

*There was also a prophet Anna . . . She was of a great age . . . She
never left the temple but worshiped there with fasting and prayer
night and day. At that moment she came, and began to praise
God and to speak about the child to all who were looking for the
redemption of Jerusalem.*

LUKE 2:36–38

In Jesus' day, Jewish parents brought their male children to the temple to be circumcised when they were eight days old. When Jesus' parents arrive for this sacred ceremony, they see an elderly, bent-over woman who regularly prays and fasts night and day. Her name is Anna and she is a prophet, who along with Simeon, immediately perceives their child to be the long-awaited Messiah of the Jewish people.

Anna then wastes no time in proclaiming this news to all who are looking for the redemption of Jerusalem. Not only is she perceptive, she is brave enough to loudly proclaim to one and all the miraculous baby she has just seen. As such, Anna is not only a prophet, she is the first evangelist in the New Testament.

While the common perception is that biblical prophets and evangelists were male, this is more Fake News. The first evangelist in the New Testament is not only female, she is also of "a great age." Today the elderly are often cast aside, viewed as if technology and time have passed them by. But in ancient times, the opposite was true. They were perceived as harbingers of truth with great wisdom. As a woman, Anna's role as both a prophet and an evangelist is distinct and rare.

Do you think anyone believed Anna when she told them a tiny baby would be the savior of their nation? I often wonder how she was received.

Have you ever known a person like Anna? What did she share with you?

After leaving the synagogue Jesus entered Simon's house. Now Simon's
mother-in-law was suffering from a high fever, and they asked him
about her. Then he stood over her and rebuked the fever, and it left her.

LUKE 4:38–39

In the gospel of Luke, the first person Jesus heals is a woman, Simon Peter's mother-in-law. In his day, most rabbis did not heal women, yet such healings were a hallmark of Jesus' ministry. Compared with other literature of the era, the New Testament contains a high number of positive references to women through depictions of Jesus' interaction with them, and it begins with his own mother.

Jesus' mother Mary is the one person who stays with Jesus from his birth to his death, the one who never leaves him. Through a mother's love, she shows him what the love of God is all about. Later described as the "first and most perfect disciple" by Pope Paul VI,[13] Mary is the first to say "yes" to God's plan for all humankind.

Along with the twelve apostles, women also followed Jesus and were thus his disciples. They provided funding for this ragtag band of followers. The movement begun by Jesus might never have left Palestine without the hands-on ministry of women.

Along with Peter's mother-in-law, Jesus also healed the woman with the flow of blood for twelve years, the daughter of the Syrophoenician woman, the woman who had been in bondage for eighteen years, the Samaritan woman at the well, Mary Magdalene, and more. Additionally, "with his absolute prohibition of divorce, Jesus gave protection to women in a society in which a husband could divorce his wife merely by giving her a legal document and sending her out of his household (see Dt 24:1–4)."[14] Jesus' protection of women against divorce was a highly significant departure from the norms of his age.

Time and again throughout Scripture, Jesus heals women and stands up for their equal treatment. Is there something instructive for you in this understanding of Jesus? Is there something instructive for us as a society?

---

13. Pope Paul VI, "Apostolic Exhortation," quoted in Brown, *The Birth of the Messiah*, 259.

14. "The Truth About Jesus," para. 13.

Soon afterwards Jesus went on through cities and villages,
proclaiming and bringing the good news of the kingdom of God. The
twelve were with him, as well as some women who had been cured of
evil spirits and infirmities: (one was) Mary, called Magdalene, from
whom seven demons had gone out . . ."

LUKE 8:1–2

Mary Magdalene is one of the first women in history to be slut-shamed. While she is universally remembered as a prostitute, nowhere in Scripture is she described as such. Not once. Yet this Fake News about Mary Magdalene has informed the dominant perception of her throughout the centuries.

Like many biblical women, she has been marginalized, her achievements have been overlooked, and in her case, falsehoods have dominated the narrative about her life. Why? Because Mary Magdalene was a powerful woman in an age when women were relegated to an inferior role. A careful reading of the gospels makes it clear that she played a central role in the life of Jesus—being healed of seven demons or unclean spirits by him, following Jesus along with the apostles, staying with him at the cross in his hour of greatest need, being among the first women to go to the tomb, and being chosen as the first to see the risen Christ.

In *Mary Magdalene: A Biography*, Dr. Bruce Chilton writes, "Mary Magdalene was the disciple who best appreciated Jesus' visionary teaching of Resurrection, and without her, Christianity would have been entirely different. It is not even clear that its core faith that Jesus' victory over the grave could have emerged without Mary."[15]

Yet throughout the centuries Mary Magdalene has been the target of projections—from being the lover in the Song of Songs, to a converted prostitute, to Jesus' concubine, to both goddess and vixen.[16] In spite of such frequent gross misrepresentations, the truth of her centrality to the Christian religion has at last been recovered; the veil has been lifted on who she really was then and who she can be for women today.

15. Chilton, *Mary Magdalene*, loc. 101.
16. Chilton, *Mary Magdalene*, loc. 140–145.

Mary Magdalene is one of many noteworthy women to be discredited by history. Do you know anyone who has suffered a similar fate? What can you do to share the True News of this person's life?

(Martha) had a sister named Mary, who sat at the LORD's feet and listened to what he was saying. But Martha was distracted by her many tasks; so she came to him and asked, "LORD, do you not care that my sister has left me to do all the work by myself? Tell her then to help me." But the LORD answered her, "Martha, Martha, you are worried and distracted by many things; there is need of only one thing. Mary has chosen the better part, which will not be taken away from her."

LUKE 10:39–42

I cannot help but wonder how Martha feels that day Jesus dines in her home. Not only has she prepared a meal for a well-known rabbi, but she has also cleaned the house, purchased ingredients, put wood in the stove, and set the table. Now there are last-minute preparations to attend to, and where is her sister Mary? Sitting at the feet of the rabbi, listening to his teaching, an activity forbidden to women. So, Martha asks Jesus to intervene because she needs help. But whose behavior does Jesus praise? Mary's.

This startling reversal of the expected female role is revealing. In Jesus' day, women were not allowed to learn. Yet he applauds Mary's decision to ditch the housework and soak up Jewish teaching. He views women as equal to men, capable of learning the sacred teachings, capable of doing more than household chores.

Not only does Jesus applaud Mary's decision, he says, "There is need of only one thing." One thing. He elevates learning to the highest responsibility of all people, women and men alike. In doing so, Jesus is not denigrating Martha's decision to tend to the kitchen chores. Instead, he is suggesting that perhaps she should take a break and learn from him as well and then her sister can help her. He seems to be saying to Martha, "You, too, can and should learn from Jewish teaching."

The adage, "With rest, you may do less but achieve more" holds true. Taking a break from the busy schedule of our lives can yield much fruit. What might happen if you heeded Jesus' advice to Martha and took a break to soak up the teachings of your Creator?

A Samaritan woman came to draw water, and Jesus said to her, "Give me a drink"... The Samaritan woman said to him, "How is that you a Jew, ask a drink of me, a woman of Samaria?"... Then the woman left her water jar and went back to the city. She said to the people, "Come and see a man who told me everything I have ever done!"... Many Samaritans from that city believed in him because of the woman's testimony.

JOHN 4:7–9, 27–28, 39

Another woman evangelist in the New Testament? Yes, this is the True News! Just as the prophet Anna recognizes Jesus as the Messiah when he is eight days old and immediately shares this news about him, so, too, does the Samaritan woman who meets Jesus at the well. Her testimony results in many believing in him, making her a significant evangelist in Scripture.

A trip to the well in Jesus' day gave women a chance to socialize as they drew bucket after bucket of water. This daily ritual took them out of their insular lives into a wider world of sharing with and learning from others. The routine was the same each day. Then suddenly Jesus enters the scene. Imagine the Samaritan woman's surprise when he engages her in conversation. Not only were men not allowed to speak to women in public, but Jews never spoke to Samaritans, due to religious differences.

During their conversation, Jesus tells her she has had five husbands and is currently living with a man to whom she is not married. The woman then recognizes Jesus as a prophet. Filled with awe at what she has been told, she immediately shares her experience and insight with everyone around her.

When Jesus breaks with tradition, recognizing the humanity of the Samaritan woman, she can see who he really is, and she becomes one of the first evangelists in the New Testament. However, she is remembered primarily for her checkered past and for the fact that Jesus dares to speak to her. The life-changing reality of her actions has been forgotten.

Today, we have a chance to applaud her insight and to rename her as an evangelist. What does this encounter reveal about Jesus' acceptance of all women, regardless of their past or present? What does this say about his desire for everyone to experience a life of spiritual truth?

How might this inform your life?

Martha said to Jesus, "LORD, if you had been here, my brother would not have died..." Jesus said to her, "Your brother will rise again." Martha said to him, "I know that he will rise again in the resurrection on the last day." Jesus said to her, "I am the resurrection and the life. Those who believe in me, even though they die, will live... Do you believe this?" She said to him, "Yes, LORD, I believe that you are the Messiah, the Son of God, the one coming into the world."

JOHN 11:21–27

How many times have I heard the plaintive cry of Martha, "If only God had done something, my loved one would not have died." Substitute the name of any person who is deeply loved—husband, wife, child, mother, father, sister, brother—and the feelings are the same. Such words are spoken out of deep pain and deep longing to see our beloved once again.

Martha's brother Lazarus has been dead for four days and, like many people in her situation, she is both grief-stricken and angry. "If you had been here, my brother would not have died," she laments, placing the blame squarely on Jesus' shoulders.

What does Jesus do? He immediately gives Martha hope by telling her that her brother will live again, somehow, through him. Then out of the depth of her darkest despair, Martha affirms that Jesus is the Messiah. Peter makes the only other verbal confession of Jesus as the Messiah, the Christ. In the first century, confessing Jesus as the Messiah was the mark of an apostle, a profound honor, yet it is Peter's confession, not Martha's, that has been highlighted in most biblical teaching.

Time and again throughout Scripture, the witness of women is recorded, but ignored historically. The evidence is right before us that women played a critical role, not only in the life of Jesus but in proclaiming him as the Messiah, the Risen One.

Let's celebrate Martha's insight into Jesus as the Christ, which places her on an equal footing with Peter. At the same time, let's do all we can to make sure the accomplishments of the marginalized in our own day are heralded and given an equal voice.

What would happen if everyone answered the call to uphold someone else? Who can you champion today?

While Pilate was sitting on the judgment seat, his wife sent word to him, "Have nothing to do with that innocent man, for today I have suffered a great deal because of a dream about him."

MATTHEW 27:19

During Jesus' trial that led to his death by crucifixion, only one person speaks out on his behalf, the wife of Pontius Pilate. Since Pilate, a Roman Governor, is the only one present who has the authority to condemn Jesus to death, her intercession could have saved his life.

I wonder how she must have felt. A woman in her culture had no standing in the law. She was the property of her husband, who was most certainly not accustomed to taking advice from her. Yet she willingly risks her relationship with her husband and her reputation to stand up for Jesus, the accused outcast.

When we stand up for the outcast, the marginalized, we can become marginalized ourselves. Taking up the cause of justice for the oppressed against the "powers that be" can result in people who once supported us turning against us. When we become one with the poor, the sick, the friendless, the accused, the imprisoned, we can be viewed as no longer part of "the group." Perhaps this is why more people are not involved in the fight for justice on a deep level. It's far easier to remain quiet and reap the benefits of a position of power, and all of us who live in the first-world have power.

Who overrides his wife's pleas for Jesus' innocence? The chief priests and elders who persuade the crowds to have Jesus killed. It is only after they become involved that the crowd shouts, "Let him be crucified."

So, this one lone woman is right, while all the chief priests and elders are wrong. What a leader. Imagine how she must have felt, especially after taking the risk that she did. Acting on her intuition, she tries to tell everyone that the proceeding is wrong, but her words go unheeded.

Have you ever had a similar experience? How did you feel?

And when they had crucified Jesus . . . Many women were also there,
looking on from a distance; they had followed Jesus from Galilee and
had provided for him. Among them were Mary Magdalene, and Mary
the mother of James and Joseph, and the mother of the sons of the
Zebedee.

MATTHEW 35:55–56

While the men flee from Jesus' crucifixion in fear, the women stead-fastly remain. Demonstrating the true nature of leadership, they do not leave him during his darkest hour. Never hesitating, never wavering, they know where they are needed and there they stay, regardless of the personal cost.

The most wonderful passage I have read about the faithfulness of these women is in *Are Women Human?* by Dorothy L. Sayers. She writes:

> Perhaps it is no wonder that the women were first at the Cradle and last at the Cross. They had never known a man like this Man—there never has been such another. A prophet and teacher who never nagged at them, never flattered or coaxed or patronized; who never made arch jokes about them, never treated them either as "The women, God help us!" or "The ladies, God bless them!"; who rebuked without querulousness and praised without condescension; who took their questions and arguments seriously, who never mapped out their sphere for them . . . There is no act, no sermon, no parable in the whole Gospel that borrows its pungency from female perversity; nobody could possibly guess from the words and deeds of Jesus that there was anything "funny" about woman's nature.[17]

One of the women who lovingly and resolutely remained at the foot of the cross was Jesus' mother Mary. The overwhelming, agonizing grief she felt did not deter her from firmly planting her feet in the ground as her son's very blood seeped into it. How she endured such unrelenting pain, I will never understand. But along with the other women, she remained.

17. Sayers, *Are Women Human?* 47.

What a gift Jesus has given to all women through the witness of his life. How important it is that this witness is not forgotten.

Is there some way you might thank him for this blessing he has given to all of us, women and men alike?

But on the first day of the week, at early dawn, the women came to the tomb, taking the spices that they had prepared. They found the stone rolled away from the tomb, but when they went in, they did not find the body. While they were perplexed about this, suddenly two men in dazzling clothes stood beside them.

LUKE 24:1–4

Amid their heartbreak, utter dejection, and defeat, expecting nothing but a lifeless form, the women rise early and go to the tomb. Even though they're perplexed and terrified, they nevertheless walk straight into the empty tomb. They walk into darkness and find light. They walk into emptiness and find fullness. They walk in alone and find angels there to guide them.

To find new life, we too must walk into the empty tomb in our lives. Whatever our spirituality, we must walk into that place where we most fear being. How we avoid these dark corners of our lives! We sometimes mask them with overwork, busy-ness, overeating, overdrinking, whatever we can find to avoid that empty tomb that resides somewhere within each one of us.

Only when we have the courage to walk right into it, will it no longer hold power over our lives. Only when we walk into the womb-like tomb, can we experience new life, rebirth.

It is significant that the women go to the tomb together. They do not go alone. When they face the darkness, they are with their sisters. They have a hand to hold, a shoulder to lean on. Together they find strength. Together they demonstrate an essential characteristic of leadership, the ability to keep going regardless of the circumstances, regardless of the uncertainty they personally feel.

Where is the empty tomb in your life? What is it that lies before you gaping in blackness and uncertainty, keeping you from the life of spiritual truth that is meant for you?

Can you, like these women, have the courage to walk in?

But Mary Magdalene stood weeping outside the tomb . . . Jesus said to her . . . "Go to my brothers and say to them, 'I am ascending to my Father and your Father, to my God and your God.'" Mary Magdalene went and announced to the disciples, "I have seen the LORD"; and she told them that he had said these things to her.

JOHN 20:11, 17–18

All four gospels identify Mary Magdalene as the first to witness the resurrection of Jesus and each one identifies her in this role. It is significant that this event, which lies at the center of the Christian faith, is recorded as having been revealed first to a woman. Not only is Mary Magdalene the first to see the risen Christ, but Jesus sends her forth to proclaim the good news to the apostles, prompting St. Bernard of Clairvaux in the thirteenth century to share the True News that Mary Magdalene was the "apostle to the apostles."

Cynthia Bourgeault writes, "a great many Christians have absorbed most of what they know about Mary Magdalene through the dual filters of tradition and the liturgy, which inevitably direct our attention toward certain aspects of the story at the expense of others."[18] What an injustice it is to all women that Mary Magdalene is not only *not* remembered as the first to see the risen Christ, but she is remembered as having been a prostitute. Nowhere in Scripture is she described as such. This Fake News has been written and spoken about Mary Magdalene for centuries, making it difficult to remember the vital role she had in the Christian story.

There was recently a cartoon circulating on social media in which Mary Magdalene and two other women are proclaiming the resurrection to the eleven male apostles. Immediately one of the apostles replies, "So ladies, thanks for being the first to witness and report the resurrection. We'll take it from here."

Of all the people who followed Jesus throughout his ministry, he chose to appear first to Mary Magdalene. In the patriarchal culture in which he lived and died, Jesus' choice speaks volumes about his view of all women and of Mary Magdalene in particular. Is there a message here for those who seek to follow Jesus today?

18. Bourgeault, "The Meaning of Mary," 6.

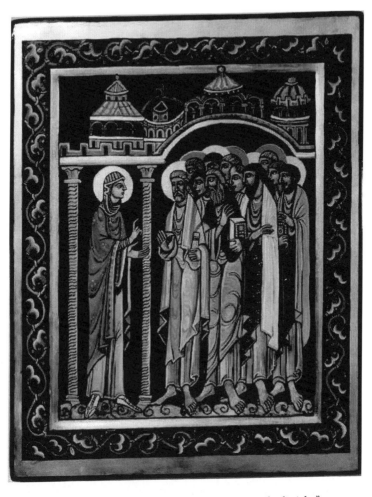

"Mary Magdalene announcing the resurrection to the disciples."
Suzanne Schleck, 2002, egg tempera and gold leaf on gessoed board, 11"x 14."
Pennsylvania, Geitz Collection.
Original in the Albani Psalter, ca. 1123. Herzog August Biliothek, Wolfenbüttel

A certain woman named Lydia, a worshiper of God, was listening to us; she was from the city of Thyatira and a dealer in purple cloth. The LORD opened her heart to listen eagerly to what was said by Paul. When she and her household were baptized, she urged us, saying, "If you have judged me to be faithful to the LORD, come and stay at my home." And she prevailed upon us.

ACTS 16:14–15

First-century Middle Eastern women had no choice but to labor in the home night and day, as tradition then dictated. True? Nope; more Fake News! Some like Lydia were successful merchants, dealers in cloth and other items. Purple was a royal color, signifying wealth. Not only was Lydia a dealer, she was a dealer in luxury goods.

She knew how to successfully handle competing demands on her time. She was a businesswoman who helped start the Christian church in Philippi and still had time to extend hospitality to Peter and Paul. How did she do it all?

We are told that the Lord opened her heart to listen eagerly to what was said by Paul. When our hearts are open, we too can receive our Divine Mother's love for us. We can begin to embrace what that means in our own lives and what it can mean to share that abundant gift with others.

With her eyes opened, Lydia reaches out far beyond her merchant's stall, far beyond her home to have a lasting impact on the world around her. Establishing a church requires time and planning, whether in a home in Philippi or in a start-up storefront today. Lydia takes that time, giving selflessly to others.

What might happen if we opened our hearts to our Divine Mother's word for us? What life-changing message could be waiting for us?

Paul . . . to all God's beloved in Rome . . . "I commend to you our sister Phoebe, a deacon of the church at Cenchreae, so that you may welcome her in the LORD as is fitting for the saints, and help her in whatever she may require from you, for she has been a benefactor of many and of myself as well."

ROMANS 1:1, 7, 16:1

In commending Phoebe, not only as his benefactor but as both sister and deacon, Paul is stating that she is equal in stature to the male leaders. The Greek word he uses for "deacon" is the same word he uses to describe himself and other leaders of the Jesus movement.

There are significantly fewer female than male leaders in America today. In 2018 less than five percent of the Fortune 500 companies had a female CEO[19], twenty-three percent of the House of Representatives and twenty-five percent of the Senate are women[20], and there has never been a female President of the United States. In some circles, the Bible is still cited as one of the reasons women should be in subordinate positions. Yet, within Scripture, there are exemplary female leaders who were well respected by their male counterparts. This is the True News that is meant to inform our understanding of the role of women in society.

There's Deborah, a judge who helped lead an army into battle; Miriam, a prophet who helped lead the exodus; the Queen of Sheba, who ruled a country; Esther, who risked her life and saved the Jewish people; Huldah, a prophet whose advice was sought by male priests; the women who stayed at the foot of the cross while every man fled; Mary Magdalene, whom the risen Jesus appeared to first; Junia named as an apostle; and more.

The belief that women cannot serve as leaders is not supported by the example of women leaders throughout Scripture. Not only does Paul introduce Phoebe to the Romans as a leader, but he bids them give her a welcome fitting of the saints. A woman deacon, leader, and saint? In the Bible? Indeed. Yet most people have never heard of her.

19. Mejia, "Just 24 Female," para. 2.
20. DeSilver, "A Record number," chart 1.

Phoebe. Remember her name. How might this first-century woman, who not only survived but thrived in a patriarchal society, inform your life?

Paul... to all God's beloved in Rome... "Greet Andronicus and Junia, my relatives who were in prison with me; they are prominent among the apostles, and they were in Christ before I was."

ROMANS 1:1, 7, 16:7

Only men were named as apostles in the Bible. Right? Wrong! More Fake News. Paul names both Junia and Andronicus apostles, a woman and man who are imprisoned along with him for their beliefs. Nowhere else in Scripture does Paul name anyone as an apostle other than himself and the original twelve. Yet here he names Junia and Andronicus as not only apostles but as prominent among them. There were not twelve apostles in the New Testament, there were fourteen.

What do we know about the only woman named as an apostle in the Bible? First, she was effective enough to be considered a threat to local authorities. Otherwise, she would not have been imprisoned along with Paul. The strength of Junia's convictions is also borne out by her willingness to go to prison for her beliefs.

Her relationship with Andronicus is not clear. Some believe they may have been a husband-wife ministry team, much like Prisca and Aquilla, but they could also have been brother and sister or related in another way. Finally, we know that Junia followed Jesus as the Christ before Paul did, so she was an early believer in Jesus as the Messiah.

What does it mean that Paul named a woman as an apostle in the first century? Does this bear any relevance for the role of women in all professions today? What could this True News mean in your life?

Prisca and Aquilla, who work with me in Christ Jesus, and who risked their necks for my life, to whom not only I give thanks, but also all the churches of the Gentiles. Greet also the church in their house.

ROMANS 16:3–5

Prisca and Aquilla travel extensively with Paul to spread the teachings of Jesus of Nazareth. As a married couple, they are equal parts of Paul's ministry team.

In the Acts of the Apostles, we are told they are tentmakers who had recently come to Corinth from Italy. The Emperor Claudius had commanded all Jews to leave Rome. Aquilla was Jewish, so, believing it was unsafe to remain in any part of Italy, Prisca and Aquilla had fled Roman persecution.

They first met Paul, also a tentmaker, in Corinth. They shared in his work and eventually led the house church there. They later traveled with him to Ephesus where they taught other leaders.

In the six times Prisca is mentioned in Scripture, she and Aquilla are always mentioned together. It is difficult to separate her work from his or even her life from his. Interestingly, in three of the six references, Prisca's name is mentioned before Aquilla's, indicating her prominence in the Pauline community as well as the prominence of women in early Christianity.

I marvel at married couples who work together day in and day out. How do they separate their work from their personal lives? Do work disagreements affect their relationship? What a model Prisca and Aquilla can be of women and men working in partnership together. How much we can learn from them.

What does it mean that over two thousand years ago Prisca was in a revered and equal partnership with her husband? How might that inform your relationships?

*Therefore, my brothers and sisters, whom I love and long for, my joy
and crown, stand firm in the LORD in this way, my beloved. I urge
Euodia and Syntyche to be of the same mind in the LORD. Yes, and I
ask you also, my loyal companion, help these women, for they have
struggled beside me in the work of the gospel.*

PHILIPPIANS 4:1–3

As women struggle for positions of leadership in corporate board-
rooms, the political arena, and religious institutions, some people
still believe that, until the 1960s, most women were content to work
only within the home.

Let me loudly proclaim, "This is Fake News!" There were numerous women leaders, not only in the Bible but in the history of
the Christian church. Euodia and Syntyche were among the women
leaders at Philippi who worked beside Paul along with Phoebe, Junia, and Prisca.

They were leaders of house churches whom Paul urges to "be
of the same mind in the Lord." This has led some to view them
as two women simply quarreling with one another. Paul is much
more likely telling them to lead their congregation with one mind
by following the teachings of Jesus. It would have been like telling
Nancy Pelosi and Alexandria Ocasio-Cortez today to not divide the
Democratic party ideologically—hardly a mere "female quarrel."

Furthermore, Biblical women leaders laid the groundwork for
female leaders in the church hundreds of years ago. In 657 CE in
England, Hilda was asked by her bishop to establish a double mon-
astery for both women and men. She did so and became the Abbot,
the head of the community, with authority over one hundred fifty
men and women. Now revered as Saint Hilda of Whitby, her role
was accepted over thirteen hundred years ago. There were other
female abbots as well who were accepted by their male and female
communities and by the church hierarchy.

How does this information make you feel? Angry at the
pervasiveness of the misconceptions we have been led to believe?
Empowered by knowledge of the history of women's biblical and
ecclesiastical leadership?

Wherever you find yourself, sit with your feelings. Can you ask your Divine Mother to join you as you strive to claim the life of spiritual truth that is yours?

Survival

"There was truth and there was untruth, and if you clung to the truth even against the whole world, you were not mad."[1]

George Orwell

"It's hard to keep my head above water these days."

2019 Facebook User

1. Orwell, *1984*, 169.

Then the woman came and told her husband, "A man of God came to me, and his appearance was like that of an angel of God, most awe-inspiring"... The angel of God came again to the woman as she sat in the field; but her husband Manoah was not with her.

JUDGES 13:6, 9

How best to keep our heads above water when we feel inundated with the Fake News that surrounds us? How to survive?

Well . . . we could become hermits, shutting ourselves off from all media, all contact with the outside world. We could listen to nothing but spa music all day. We could refuse to interact on any level with anyone who disagrees with us on the topic *du jour*. But such extreme measures are not the answer for most of us.

The truth is, the Bible, the very book that has been twisted and used against women, blacks, gays, Jews, and those from other countries, contains some of the most comforting words ever written. Let's look at some of those passages.

When an angel appears to Manoah's wife, she is in a field by herself, away from her everyday existence. The angel does not come to her during her many daily chores, but, instead, when she takes time to be apart, away from life's distractions. Sitting in the field alone, she hears the message that she will conceive and bear a son, a long-awaited dream.

Perhaps her field was what some people today describe as a thin place, "where only tissue paper separates the material from the spiritual."[2] On a recent pilgrimage to one of the thin places, the Isle of Iona in Scotland, I was unexpectedly overwhelmed by a strong sense of the Divine Spirit's presence.

Sitting on a hard chair in the cold Abbey of Iona, I suddenly felt a presence so powerful I had an urge to flee. Instead, I willed myself to stay and listen, listen with the ear of the heart. In the stillness and solitude, the Spirit's message for me was clear, filling my body and soul with a sense of peace and unity with all creation, filling me with spiritual truth and fulfillment so longed for.

When the prevalence of misleading, contradictory news reports gets you down, what if you took some time away from the

2. Macleod, Iona Abbey, Scotland.

24-hour news cycle? Away from the distractions of our noisy world? The good news is we don't have to be in a "thin place" to communicate with the Divine Spirit. We can be on a retreat, in our backyard, even in our own homes.

What might happen if you turned off all electronics, went to a quiet spot, and put yourself in the Spirit's presence?

What do you need, right now, to fill your soul with the gift of the spirit of truth that is yours?

You have turned my mourning into dancing; you have taken off my
sackcloth and clothed me with joy, so that my soul may praise you
and not be silent. O LORD my God, I will give thanks to you forever.

PSALM 30:11–12

"The world is often a difficult place, full of fear and anger and suffering. But it is important to see that love and joy also fill our world. I share this belief with one of my closest and most mischievous friends, His Holiness the Dalai Lama. I am asking you to help us show that the world is not beyond hope. Anger, fear, and despair. No! These will not have the last word."[3]

So begins a video message from Desmond Tutu, the retired Anglican Archbishop of South Africa. What balm it is to the soul to hear his words in today's world. When article after article, post after post are filled with gloom and doom, dire predictions, hate and fear, we can almost forget that this is only partial truth.

Every day thousands of acts of kindness occur between loved ones, friends, and strangers alike. Every day a doctor saves a life, EMT personnel perform life-saving measures; police and firefighters risk their lives to respond to emergency calls. Every day a teacher goes the extra mile to help a child who is falling behind, and aid workers go into high-risk situations in war-torn nations to reach out to the homeless, refugees, a distressed parent, or a hurt child. Every day the naked are clothed, the hungry are fed, the sick are visited, the wounded are healed, and someone receives another chance at life.

Every day an electrician repairs a power grid, and a plumber keeps the water flowing. Every day someone works the extra hour with no pay because that is what's needed, and a young person receives mentoring from a wiser, more experienced, loving soul. Every day clergy take time to listen, to care, and to reach out in the name of God to those in desperate need of a healing word. Every day people donate to charities with myriad goals to help someone they will never meet. Every day cross-cultural relationships among people of different cultures and traditions are changing our world one child, one person at a time.

3. Tutu, Share The Joy video, Facebook.

Every day a child is born and parents, grandparents, and loved ones shed tears of indescribable joy. Every day someone says, "I love you" and means it with all their heart and soul. Every day someone is comforted, hugged, and told they are special beyond measure.

Every single day without exception. This is the True News! Love and joy. It's all around. Can you feel it?

*Where you go, I will go; where you lodge, I will lodge; your people
shall be my people, and your God my God.*

RUTH 1:16

In the Celtic tradition, there is a concept known as *anam cara*, which means "soul love" or "soul friend." When we are with our *anam cara*, there is no mask, no pretense, nothing superficial. It is a friendship in which we feel truly understood, truly at home. With such understanding comes a sense of belonging at the deepest level, enabling us to enter a unity of sacred belonging, a belonging that began long before we were born.[4]

When you have an *anam cara*, friendship cuts across all convention and category. You are joined in an ancient and eternal way with the friend of your soul. From a position of such deep connectedness, we can truly discover who we are and delight in the other. We can also be empowered to accomplish that which we could never accomplish on our own.

In the Bible, Naomi and Ruth have that soul friendship that transcends time and space and boundaries. The above passage is often read at weddings, although the words are spoken by Ruth to her mother-in-law, Naomi. The message they contain, however, is timeless and transcends the boundaries of only one type of relationship.

Naomi and Ruth are widows who need each other's protection to survive in a patriarchal society. Ruth is a foreigner in an alien land and needs Naomi for her acceptance, and Naomi needs Ruth's youth and vigor. But the unbreakable bond of a soul friendship nurtures them both and binds them together for all time.

In our increasingly uncertain world, we all need the anchor of a spiritual friend. Many people have an *anam cara* of whom they are not aware. Do you have one? If not, could you ask your Creator for the gift of recognition?

4. O'Donohue, *Anam Cara*, 17.

As a deer longs for flowing streams, so my soul longs for you,
O God.

PSALM 42:1

What can we do when we're feeling weighed down by the preponderance of Fake News? What can we do when we're barely keeping our heads above water?

Living in the mountains of Pennsylvania, my husband and I often see deer sauntering up to our pond for a drink of cool water. They come back again and again. Once is never enough. How blessed they are to have found the sustenance they seek.

In his book *Something More*, John Pritchard shares, "I write in the belief that 'God' keeps leaking into our lives but that we have difficulty finding the language to describe the experience. I think many of us have intimations of 'something more,' something that might even have on it the fingerprints of a divine Source, but how can we admit that or pursue it further?"[5]

Do you long for a satisfaction deep in your soul that seems just out of reach, a connectedness yearned for but unfulfilled? If so, you are not alone. Some people try to fill this emptiness with work, others with alcohol, drugs, serial relationships, or frequent job changes. Advertisers prey on this sense of need, promising fulfillment if only we purchase their product. This misinformation permeates our newsfeed and airwaves. Yet, regardless of our actions, at the end of the day, there is still the aching feeling that there's something more just around the corner.

"You have made us for yourself, O Lord, and our heart is restless until it rests in you." Written by Augustine over sixteen hundred years ago, these words are profound. Our hearts are indeed restless until we connect with our Divine Mother or Cosmic Energy. Whatever words we use to describe the reality of "something more," the reality is the same and, once we tap into that, our lives can be changed forever.

How to do that? We can sit quietly and meditate. Or we can open our eyes to the Divine in our midst every day—in the majestic beauty of a sunset, the smile on a child's face, the friend who is

5. Pritchard, *Something More*, 4.

always there, the encouraging word spoken to us at just the right time. Our Creator is all around us, hoping our hearts will rest in her divine embrace.

Where do you see "something more?" Can you rest there, even for a moment?

Be still and know that I am God.

Be still and know that I am God. Be still and know that I am. Be still and know. Be still. Be.

Whenever I am not sure how to communicate with our Divine Mother, the words of this psalm come to mind. Whether you think of it as a mantra, a chant, or a prayer, the words can slowly draw us in and toward something larger than ourselves. Repeated over and over they can put us in touch with the Divine Energy that dwells within each one of us.

Connecting with the Divine doesn't always involve our talking, sharing our needs, wants or desires. Our Creator knows far better than we do what we need. One of the most important aspects of being in any relationship is to listen, and our Creator wants nothing less from us.

Recently, as I began praying, I heard in my mind, "Please stop talking and listen to me." That brought me up short! So, I stopped talking and listened. I was still. Becoming aware of the rhythm of my breathing, I began to sense our Divine Mother's message for me. While the specific message will be different for each of us, if it is from the Divine, it will have one thing at its core. Love.

The Most Rev. Michael Curry, Presiding Bishop of the Episcopal Church, is fond of saying, "If it's not about love, it's not about God." How true that statement is. If we believe our Creator is urging us to say, or post, or tweet, or do something that isn't about love, then it is not of God. Best to hit the delete key!

Love is the very essence of God's being, prompting Augustine to write of the three-fold nature of God as Lover, Beloved, and the Love that Exists Between Them. While not an official trinitarian designation, it is nonetheless one of my favorites.

Be still and know that I am God. Be still and know that I am. Be still and know. Be still. Be.

Bless the LORD, O my soul. O LORD my God, you are very great.
You are clothed with honor and majesty, wrapped in light as with
a garment. . .You make springs gush forth in the valleys; they flow
between the hills. . .By the streams the birds of the air have their
habitation; they sing among the branches.

PSALM 104:1, 10–12

The whole world is aflutter with tweets. Some attacking, some informing. Some bullying, some encouraging. Some transparent, some obfuscating. Some trolling, some genuine. Many purposefully attracting attention. Those written to garner headlines never fail to do so, from the original tweet to the multitude of pithy and often snarky responses. Regardless of where we find ourselves on the political spectrum, many of us find this behavior troublesome at best, defaming of our country at worst.

Yet we continue to read and respond, easily manipulated by those pulling the strings. The more we cry "foul," the more we continue to engage, becoming addicted to the outrageous, the unthinkable, the whims of politicians, celebrities, anyone in the public eye. Is there an antidote? A way out of the rabbit hole? Of course! There always is. We just need to find it, pursue it, and cultivate it.

Last week I could not listen to one more piece of Breaking News. So, I escaped to my backyard and took a print book instead of my ever-present iPad with Kindle app. As I read the book in my hands and turned the pages, savoring the feel of them, I gradually noticed the sounds of nature all around me. All God's creatures heralded their presence with splashing, croaking, gobbling, grunting, chattering, and, you guessed it—tweeting. Two birds began having a "conversation." One to my right, high in an overhead branch, trilled excitedly. Then one to my left, in the bulrushes, responded in kind. Soon they were excitedly communicating with one another in melodious song.

When the excitement passed, their pace slowed. Soothing tweets filled the air, lulling me to sleep, filled with an awareness of my oneness with nature, filled with a sense of connection to something much larger than myself. Just before nodding off, I felt that peace that passes all understanding that is pure gift from God.

Feelings of "all is right with the world" enveloped me, hugging me in warm embrace.

The depth of that oneness with creation will stay with me a long time. When I'm tempted to become embroiled in the circus created by the 24-hour news media, I remember the stark contrast between real tweets and social media tweets, and I recall a meal blessing I recently taught our four-year-old granddaughter:

Thank you for the world so sweet.
Thank you for the food we eat.
Thank you for the birds that sing.
Thank you, God, for everything.
Amen.

What might happen if we spent as much time listening to real "tweets," as we do to those on social media?

And Jesus came and said to them . . . "Remember, I am with you always to the end of the age."

MATTHEW 28: 18, 20

Jesus' final message to his followers is one of both protection and power. He, and therefore the Divine Spirit, is with us always—not just when we are perfect, not just when we've got it all figured out. Always. When we completely ruin everything, lose our temper royally, or fail miserably, the Spirit is with us. When we grieve, rejoice, or lose all hope, the Spirit is with us.

An oil painting hangs in St. Mary's Episcopal Cathedral in Edinburgh, Scotland that is both startling and comforting in its revelation. In the north choir aisle, beside the organ there is an artist's rendering of the cathedral with Holy Communion taking place at the main altar. In the foreground, behind the cathedral chairs, there is a widow dressed in black, on her knees praying and overcome with grief, unable to join the others. Standing right behind her is the gossamer presence of Jesus, blessing and comforting her.[6]

Knowing that we have a source of Divine Energy with us all day in every way can be comforting. It can also be empowering. Those who fight for justice are not alone. Those who work for peace, for the oppressed, and for the marginalized are not alone. Those who march for climate change are not alone, and the list goes on. When a breakthrough never seems to come and we are ready to give up, we are not alone. The Spirit is beside us, behind us, and over us, working along with us.

In what aspect of your life do you need to draw on this source of Divine Energy? Could you try? Right now?

6. Borthwick, *The Presence*, Scotland.

"I have come that they may have life, and have it abundantly."

JOHN 10:10

During Jesus' time on earth, he often tries in vain to explain what it means to embrace the way of love that he came to proclaim, what it means to live a life of loving your neighbor as yourself, welcoming the stranger, healing the sick, visiting the imprisoned, and caring for young and old alike.

Finally, one day, almost in exasperation, he sums it up, "It's about having abundant life! It's about living the life of spiritual abundance that is freely given to you. It's right here. All you have to do is accept it." I can almost feel his frustration when people still do not understand the meaning of his words. Instead of acceptance, many are saying, "He has a demon and is out of his mind. Why listen to him?" (John 10:20).

When something is too good to be true, we often decide there must be a catch somewhere. The adage, "When it's too good to be true, it usually is," comes to mind.

Our Creator longs for you and me to live the life of spiritual truth that is ours for the taking. Yet so many obstacles can stand in the way of this, and one is the prevalence of news that blurs or outright distorts the truth.

Fake News can distract us, confuse us, wear us down. It's easy to feel overwhelmed and like giving up. When we feel that way, let us remember the example Jesus set for us. He often took time to be apart, to pray or to reflect, to be in nature, where he was nurtured by the beauty of creation.

We are all meant to live a life of spiritual truth, each one of us. What do you need to do to embrace spiritual truth in your own life?

Do not be conformed to this world, but be transformed by the renewing of your minds, so that you may discern what is the will of God—what is good and acceptable and perfect.

ROMANS 12:2

A common theme throughout Scripture is that people of faith must be *in* the world, but not *of* the world. What does this mean for those of us who seek truth, justice, and equality for all? It means that, while we may not have a choice but to live in a world that has been powered by the engine of patriarchy since the beginning of time, we do not have to accept that system as normative.

It means that we can be transformed by the renewing of our minds and that we can seek to transform others. The 2017 Women's March on Washington and around the world is a stellar example of such activity. Estimated at up to five million people worldwide, it was held in support of women's rights, LGBT rights, gender and racial equality, worker rights, disability rights, and more. Around the world, women collectively rose up together and said, "No more!" And slowly, ever so slowly, change is beginning to happen.

Nothing we do to contribute to this change is too small. I often think of the books I write as a drop of water on a rock—drip, drip, drip until gradually the rock begins to erode. One drip at a time. One step at a time. One day at a time, we will get there. Together.

What gifts has your Creator given you? Do you feel drawn to express yourself through writing, speaking, organizing, listening, working behind the scenes, meeting in small groups, joining with sisters, marching? Where is our Divine Mother leading you? Listen to that small voice within . . . then act.

The transformation of ourselves and our world does not happen in a vacuum. It is most often the result of painstakingly hard work, either personally or in the public arena.

Where might you be called to act? Is there something holding you back?

We are afflicted in every way, but not crushed; perplexed, but not driven to despair; persecuted, but not forsaken; struck down, but not destroyed.

2 CORINTHIANS 4:8–9

Octavio Lizarde, who witnessed his nephew die in the 2019 El Paso shooting massacre, said, "It's hard because he was like my son. I was always there for him when he needed it—and it hurts . . . Just those images that I saw. I really wish I didn't see them. I close my eyes. I still see them. I see them open. I see everything."[7]

Paul tells us in Second Corinthians that there are times in our lives when we may be struck down, but that in those times we are not destroyed, regardless of how devastated we may feel. How easy this is to forget when we are feeling persecuted, struck down, or at our lowest.

Can you remember a time when you felt that way? Have you ever been the target of a racist, sexist, heterosexist, or anti-Semitic attack? Have you ever been brought to your knees by a stranger's hatred for you simply because of how God created you? Or by a friend who didn't value you as you thought they did?

We can have hope for a new tomorrow if we can remember that our Creator loves us especially when we are at our lowest and feeling that our emotional scars will never heal.

Prize-winning author Amy Ferris is fond of saying, "Wear your scars like stardust." She adds, "I think scars—whether they're physical, or emotional—are signs of huge massive bravery and courage. They often mean that someone has come through, walked through, run through, the fire."[8] How brilliantly she turns a deep wound, either physical or emotional, into something beautiful.

American gospel artist Mandisa lyrically portrays how God can use our scars for the good in, "That's What Scars Are For," from her Grammy award-winning album, *Overcomer*.[9]

7. Keneally and Hutchinson, "Victims of Dayton," para. 42.

8. Yerman, "Amy Ferris," para. 11.

9. Mandisa, "That's What Scars Are For," https://www.youtube.com/watch?v=7Gvt__r9EU0.

Whether we or a loved one have ever been the victim of an attack, we all have scars of one kind or another. Each one of us.

How might you turn your scars into stardust? How might you use them to help others?

Let all of us speak the truth to our neighbors, for we are members of one another.

EPHESIANS 4:25

"Be the change that you wish to see in the world." These well-known words of Mahatma Gandhi ring true throughout the ages. People often lament that the world is not as they wish it to be, nor as it could be. As we read one news item after another filled with lies and see serial prevaricators maintaining positions of power, we can feel helpless to change anything.

And the truth is, on one level we *are* helpless. We cannot change someone else. This is universally true. We cannot change anyone other than ourselves, not even (and especially) those closest to us.

While we can denounce what we see in our leaders or in those around us, while we can protest and sign petitions, we cannot ultimately change someone else's behavior. But we can change ourselves. We can take our power back by refusing to be consumed in fruitless attempts to change the other. We can stand firm in our convictions of who we are, with whom we wish to associate, whom we will vote for, and more.

And yes, we can speak the truth to our neighbors, for we are indeed members of one another. I have found it increasingly difficult to speak truth to those who have a radically different worldview than do I. But nothing is more important than that we stay in dialogue at some level with those very people.

For the sake of self-preservation, we don't need to be in dialogue with everyone who disagrees with us, but cutting ourselves off completely from those with a different perspective is not good for anyone, including ourselves, for we are indeed members of one another.

Is there one person with whom you might dialogue who disagrees with you on various issues? Is there someone with whom our Creator might be calling you to engage? Meditate and reflect on this. It isn't easy.

If someone comes to mind, remember how important it is to listen. We cannot expect others to listen to us if we will not listen to them. Pray for our Divine Mother to give you strength, wisdom, and the words to share with this person.

Can you be the change you wish to see in this world?

Finally, beloved, whatever is true, whatever is honorable, whatever is just, whatever is pure, whatever is pleasing, whatever is commendable, if there is any excellence and if there is anything worthy of praise, think about these things.

PHILIPPIANS 4:8

What is the best way to deal with Fake News, distressing True News, and one disturbing headline after another? As much as we might sometimes wish to, we can't take a permanent break from it. To do so would be to relinquish our rights and neglect our responsibilities as citizens in the country and world we all hold dear. No, we must stay informed. We must act, but we must also take a break from the news when that's what we need.

I recently returned from a Celtic Pilgrimage in Scotland and England. One of the greatest gifts to me on that journey is that I had no news. Suddenly I was unplugged, in nature all day instead of in front of one screen or another. That was incredibly healing, and, upon my return, I found my appetite for news had lessened. My commitment to fighting injustice was just as strong, but the incessant news from a variety of sources no longer fed my spirit.

There are times in our lives when we need to focus on and bask in whatever is true, whatever is honorable, whatever is just and pure. In doing so, we are renewed for the task that lies before us. In doing so, we are refreshed as we dwell in the beauty of creation as it was meant to be enjoyed.

When upsetting news assaults our senses, let us focus on that which is good. There is so much goodness in the world. Many people are going the extra mile to help a stranger in need. As Mr. Rogers told his young television neighbors, "When I was a boy and I would see scary things in the news, my mother would say to me, 'Look for the helpers. You will always find people who are helping.'"

To Mr. Rogers' timely words, I add, "Look for the resisters. Look for those who persist and resist." Look for the bright light amid the darkness. It is there. Our Divine Creator is there. Rest in the knowledge that goodness is out there; then we will be renewed to continue our struggle to right the wrongs that assault our senses.

Pray without ceasing.

1 THESSALONIANS 5:16

Yes, it can be difficult to watch the news. Grim scenes, raw grief etched into people's faces, events that spiral out of control while more people, communities, and countries are harmed—that's the True News we fervently wish we could change.

A mentor of mine, now deceased, had a never-fail remedy for dealing with bad news. Her name was Sister Lorette Piper, better known as "Retsy" to those who knew and loved her—and we were many. Retsy introduced me to what became five and a half years of work in inner-city Trenton, New Jersey with women struggling to make it off welfare. Each month a group of us who worked there met to make sense of what we were experiencing and feeling.

One night, after a particularly rough day of news, Retsy told us, "Pray the news! Try it!" These three words can completely change the way we hear the news. Thank goodness I remembered her wisdom last week and, yes, I had forgotten her sage advice.

So yesterday, my news viewing was more like this:

Most gracious God, please be with each person who mourns the death of a beloved friend, family member, or stranger from the hands of yet another mass shooter in Texas. Be especially with the parents of the seventeen-month old girl who was shot in the face today. Their pain, their grief, is overwhelming. Their questions and our questions continue hauntingly into the night as we wonder why nothing seems to change. Comfort them in their deep sorrow. Divine Mother, give our politicians the wisdom, courage, and strength to enact the laws that can save countless lives in the days and years to come. Open their hearts to be moved by the suffering they see. Let them feel the pain and hear the cries of these wounded souls.

Loving Creator, your children in the Anglophone region of Cameroon, West Africa continue to suffer. For three years they have not been able to attend school due to armed conflict in the region between their people and the Francophone government. For three years international bodies have called for ceasefire and inclusive dialogue with a third-party mediator, yet the government has ignored their calls. For three years, the United Nations has not stepped in to save the lives of blameless women, men, and children. Why do I live in safety, when so many of my sisters and brothers do not have that luxury? Help me to learn to love the questions themselves.

Ah! Some good news at last. God our Mother and Father, thank you for the ad featuring a model in a wheelchair that lit up the face of four-year-old Maren Anderson when she saw it. Maren has a rare disease caused by a genetic mutation and recently started using a wheelchair. Understandably sensitive to the many changes in her life, her countenance was changed in an instant when she found herself portrayed by a model. Inclusivity can change the world one person at a time. Thank you, gracious God, for the joy such awareness brings. May this awareness spread to the farthest corners of the world.

God, I put every one of your children in the news today in your loving hands. I know you can do infinitely more for them than I can even ask or imagine.

What could it be like for you to "pray the news" every day?

*Proclaim the message; be persistent whether the time is favorable
or unfavorable; convince, rebuke, and encourage, with the utmost
patience in teaching. For the time is coming when people will not put
up with sound doctrine, but having itching ears, they will accumulate
for themselves teachers to suit their own desires, and will turn away
from listening to the truth and wander away to myths.*

2 TIMOTHY 2:2-4

Are these words really from the Bible or were they written last week? They ring so true, so descriptive of our age that it is almost eerie. Yet, it is also comforting.

What we are experiencing in America right now has happened before and will happen again. People have "itching ears!" The word translated as "itch" here means "to itch, rub, scratch, or tickle." People prefer their ears tickled with fanciful sayings and stories rather than with words of truth. They want political speeches and sermons and teachers who tell them what they want to hear and desperately want to believe, rather than what is true and what is best for the common good.

I love the many timeless universal truths contained within Scripture—truths that are just as relevant today as they were when they were written. Our current feelings of helplessness, of being perplexed by how we got here have a basic answer that is seldom mentioned—human nature. It is human nature for some people to grasp on to what they want to hear and want to believe and to hold tightly to that belief almost as if their lives depended on it, because at some deep level they believe it does.

In helping Timothy address a problem within his church community, Paul articulates a clear way out of the serious issues that occur when people "turn away from listening to the truth and wander away to myths."

"Proclaim the message! Be persistent, whether the time to do so is favorable or not! Convince, rebuke, and encourage! And most of all, be patient in your teaching." And what is the message? Love your neighbor as yourself—all neighbors, whether they look like you, love like you, believe as you, or, yes, vote like you. All neighbors. No exceptions.

If we stay on message, if we never give up proclaiming it, regardless of the circumstances, regardless of how worn down we may become, this time will not last. It will not last. Our Creator, and those who follow this divine, loving energy have shown us the way.

Will you follow?

You will know the truth, and the truth will make you free.

JOHN 8:32

The Milford Readers and Writers Festival held each fall in Milford, Pennsylvania inspires conversations between people who love to read books and people who write them. Featured authors have spanned the gamut from internationally known mystery authors to those who write about the afterlife to former CIA agents.

One recent panel featured Pulitzer-prize winning author Tim Weiner and former Acting Director of Operations of the Central Intelligence Agency, Jack Devine. Weiner's book, *Legacy of Ashes: The History of the CIA* is the book the CIA does not want you to read.[10] Devine's book, *Good Hunting: An American Spymaster's Story,* is a testament to the CIA.[11] Both highly trained professional men saw the same "truth," yet came to very different conclusions about it.

Etched into the walls of the original CIA headquarters building in Washington, D.C. are the following words:

"And ye shall know the truth and the truth shall set you free." John VIII–XXXII

This passage from Scripture characterizes the intelligence mission in a free society—gathering intelligence, gathering the truth about those who would do us harm, in this instance harm to the United States of America.

But the truth seems to be elusive right now, not only between America and foreign powers but between Americans themselves. The partisan divide has not been as deep as it is now since the years immediately following the Civil War.

Where does that leave us? I believe it leaves us with an obligation to do everything we personally can to discern the truth of a story before we tell it, the truth of a post before we post or re-post it on social media, the truthfulness of the person who is telling us something but might be lying to us. And this is seldom easy. It takes

10. Weiner, *Legacy of Ashes.*
11. Devine, *Good Hunting.*

discernment. It takes time. It takes perseverance. It takes a commitment to our own truthfulness to others.

For me personally, it also takes a commitment to a higher truth, one that informs my life day in and day out—that there is a Divine Energy, a Creator, who is the ultimate arbiter of truth, who knows what the truth is, a truth that someday will be revealed to each one of us.

One of my favorite passages in all of Scripture is in Paul's First Letter to the Corinthians, "For now we see in a mirror, dimly, but then we will see face to face. Now I know only in part; then I will know fully, even as I have been fully known" (1 Cor 13:12).

Yes, some day we shall indeed know the truth and that truth shall set us free.

And Pilate asked him [Jesus], "What is truth?"

JOHN 18:38

This is the burning question of our time, isn't it? What is truth? What is True News and what isn't?

With the prevalence of social media, bogus news sources are everywhere, urging us to believe half-truths or outright lies. How to separate fact from fiction? Very carefully—in community, in reflection, and after much discernment.

But there is good news. Today, we know not to take everything we read at face value. We know to question, to check, and double-check everything.

Yet for centuries, we had no clue we had to do that with the Bible. We did not realize that the words we were reading were, in fact, translations of original Hebrew and Greek texts, in many cases based on incomplete manuscripts. We did not realize that esteemed scholars did not always agree on a given translation, and no one informed us that, as later manuscripts were discovered, our biblical translations would of necessity evolve and change.

While the King James Version of the Bible is still the most popular translation by far, it contains numerous inaccuracies. Why have you never heard of the feminine images of God revealed in *Spiritual Truth in the Age of Fake News*? Because you won't find most of them in the King James Version.

It took women becoming theologians, rabbis, priests, and ministers to uncover and recover these lost Scriptural passages so vital to our understanding of ourselves as women. I am thankful that day has arrived. I am thankful that we now have accurate translations and that both women and men participate in the arduous task of translating and interpreting ancient scriptures.

What is truth? It is right in front of us. For biblical scholars, it took centuries to get here, but the good news is that with the New Revised Standard Version (NRSV) of the Bible, used in this book, our long wait is over. A life of spiritual truth is right here for all of us.

In terms of secular news, our journey is just beginning. Here, I also believe, it will take the careful work of women and men, gays and straights, people of all races and all religions working together to sort fact from fiction.

The example has been set. Let us all follow it together.

Epilogue

How best to forge a new path together based on sound biblical scholarship? By embracing several core principles.

First, over eight hundred biblical manuscripts were not discovered until the late 1940s. Known as the Dead Sea Scrolls, they were unearthed over three hundred years after the King James Version of the Bible was translated, and they include almost the only surviving biblical documents written pre-second century. As a result, any translation before the 1940s is inaccurate.

Second, the original biblical manuscripts were written in Hebrew and Greek. Every Bible we read in the English language is a translation, some better than others. Translators of the New Revised Standard Version, published in 1989 by the National Council of Churches, include scholars representing Catholic, Protestant, and Orthodox Christian groups as well as Jewish representatives responsible for the Hebrew Bible/Old Testament. The NRSV is the version preferred by biblical scholars today. Choose your translation wisely.

Third, as biblical scholar Ellen F. Davis states, "we must do justice to other readers with whom we share texts, seeking to engage them in reasoned, often deeply argued conversations about particular texts and their possible meanings"—with Jews and Christians, secularists and traditionalists, our contemporaries and past generations.[1]

1. Davis, *Opening Israel's Scriptures,* loc. 201.

Fourth, all passages of Scripture must be read in context. Proof-texting has never been a viable method of biblical interpretation. Almost anything can be proven by quoting Scripture out of context. As discussed in chapter 4, William Sloan Coffin wrote that those who do so are not biblical literalists, but selective literalists, who cite only those passages that confirm their belief or agenda.[2]

Selective literalism has led to the abuse of using Scripture to proclaim women as inferior, promote slavery, condemn homosexuality, turn away the stranger, promote a culture of fear rather than love, and more. Selective literalism has become the fallback position for those who do not understand the depth and breadth of the biblical witness.

Traditional fundamentalism not only holds blind obedience to a male hierarchy that often claims to speak for God, but it also exhibits a disdain for rational, intellectual inquiry.[3] It is this disdain for a scholarly approach to biblical interpretation that has led to the abuse of Scripture and the promotion of an agenda that is not supported by what the Bible actually says. Let us not shun but embrace what the last eighty years of biblical scholarship can teach us.

How can we correctly interpret Scripture when there are basic tensions within it? By letting the Bible critique itself. Biblical scholar Walter Brueggemann has stated, "Martin Luther King Jr. famously said that the arc of history is bent toward justice. And the parallel statement that I want to make is that the arc of the Gospel is bent toward inclusiveness . . . That's the elemental conviction through which I then read the text."[4] The entire trajectory of Scripture points to our Creator's inclusive love for all people, and ultimately Scripture must be interpreted through this lens which is supported by the foundational biblical stories—creation and the exodus in the Hebrew Bible/Old Testament and the life and teachings of Jesus in the New Testament.

In Genesis, God creates the earth and all that is in it out of overflowing love. God cannot be God without love, and we are, every one of us, made in God's image. No one is excluded. There is

2. Coffin, *Credo,* 159.
3. Hedges, *American Fascists,* 13.
4. Wortman, "The Gospel vs. Scripture?" para. 9.

nothing in either creation story giving one sex or one race dominion over the other.

And the defining story of the Israelites? The exodus. God hears the cries of the enslaved Israelites and sides, not with the Pharaoh, not with the wealthy ruling class, but with the oppressed. The dominant Hebrew Bible/Old Testament themes are of a Creator of radically inclusive love who sides with the oppressed. Every other verse of Scripture must be interpreted in that light.

Christians correctly interpret Scripture through one lens—the life and teachings of Jesus. Jesus could not have made it clearer that he came to teach us to welcome the stranger, feed the hungry, clothe the naked, and visit the prisoner. He could not have been clearer regarding the status of women when time and again he healed women when other rabbis of his time would not. He could not have been clearer when he chose to appear first to a woman, Mary Magdalene, following his resurrection.

In answer to the Pharisee who asked Jesus which commandment in the law is the greatest, his answer could not have been clearer. "'You shall love the Lord your God with all your heart, and with all your soul, and with all your mind'. This is the greatest and first commandment. And a second is like unto it: 'You shall love your neighbor as yourself'. On these two commandments hang all the law and the prophets" (Matt 22:37–40).

Love your neighbor as yourself. All neighbors. No one is excluded. It really is that simple.

About the Author

Elizabeth Geitz's books have been hailed by people as diverse as Archbishop Desmond Tutu, Sister Helen Prejean, and John Berendt. Focusing on spirituality and justice issues, her writings speak to people of passion who long to make a difference in the world.

Elizabeth is an Episcopal priest and canon, award-winning author, and non-profit entrepreneur. As the founder of Good Shepherd Sustainable Learning Foundation, www.ImaginingTomorrow.org, she has joined hands with Sister Jane Mankaa in a cross-cultural partnership to build Good Shepherd Academy in Cameroon, West Africa, a coed residential secondary/high school for 350 students. Among other subjects, the principles contained in *Spiritual Truth in the Age of Fake News* are taught to students there in an atmosphere of inclusivity and justice.

Visit her at www.ElizabethGeitz.com and join with others in blog discussions. She would love to hear from you!

Bibliography

Agrawal, Priya. "Maternal mortality and morbidity in the United States of America." *Bulletin of the World Health Organization,* n.d. https://www.who.int/bulletin/volumes/93/3/14-148627/en/.

Amazon Editorial Review. "Q and A with author Matthew Vines." n.d. https://www.amazon.com/God-Gay-Christian-Biblical-Relationships-ebook/dp/B00F1W0RD2.

Amnesty International. "Another year, another unarmed black man killed by police." 2009. https://www.amnestyusa.org/another-year-another-unarmed-black-man-killed-by-police/.

Amnesty International. "The US Maternal Health Crisis: 14 Numbers You Need to Know." n.d. https://www.amnestyusa.org/the-u-s-maternal-health-crisis-14-numbers-you-need-to-know/.

Andone, Dakin. "In the past 6 weeks, churches, a synagogue, and mosques have been attacked." *CNN World,* April 29, 2019. https://www.cnn.com/2019/04/28/world/san-diego-synagogue-christchurch-mosque-sri-lanka-church/index.html.

Arndt, William F. and F. Wilbur Gingrich. Cited in *A Greek English Lexicon of the New Testament and Other Early Christian Literature.* Chicago: University of Chicago Press, 1957.

Associated Press. "Robertson Letter Attacks Feminists." *The New York Times,* August 26, 1992.

Baloch, Babar. "UNHCR says funds urgently needed for displaced Cameroonians," March 26, 2019. https://www.unhcr.org/en-us/news/briefing/2019/3/5c99e8254/unhcr-says-funds-urgently-needed-displaced-cameroonians.html.

Bessey, Sarah. *Jesus Feminist: God's Radical Notion that Women are People Too.* Great Britain: Darton, Longman, and Todd, 2013.

BGEA Staff. "Why does the Bible refer to God in masculine terms?" n.d. https://billygraham.org/answer/why-does-the-bible-refer-to-god-in-masculine-terms/.

Borthwick, Capt. A. E. *The Presence,* 1910, oil on canvas, St. Mary's Episcopal Cathedral, Edinburgh, Scotland.

Bosman, Julie, et al. "A Common Trait Among Mass Killers: Hatred Toward Women." *The New York Times,* August 10, 2019. https://www.nytimes.com/2019/08/10/us/mass-shootings-misogyny-dayton.html.

Bourgeault, Cynthia. *The Meaning of Mary Magdalene: Discovering the Woman at the Heart of Christianity.* Boston: Shambhala, 2010.

Brakeman, Lyn. *God Is Not A Boy's Name: Becoming Woman, Becoming Priest.* Eugene, OR: Cascade, 2016.

Brazell, Emma. "Greta Thunberg says being different is a 'superpower' in emotional post online." *Metro,* September 1, 2019. https://metro.co.uk/2019/09/01/greta-thunberg-says-being-different-is-a-superpower-in-emotional-post-online-10666558/.

Brown, Raymond. *The Birth of the Messiah: A Commentary on the Infancy Narratives in Matthew and Luke.* New York: Doubleday, 1977.

Bussie, Jacqueline Aileen. *Love Without Limits: Jesus' Radical Vision for Love with No Exceptions.* Minneapolis: Fortress, 2018.

Bynum, Caroline Walker. *Jesus as Mother: Studies in the Spirituality of the High Middle Ages.* Berkeley: University of California Press, 1982.

Carroll, Linda. "LGBT youth at higher risk for suicide attempts." *Reuters,* October 8, 2018. https://www.reuters.com/article/us-health-lgbt-teen-suicide/lgbt-youth-at-higher-risk-for-suicide-attempts-idUSKCN1MI1SL.

Center for American Progress. "How Predatory Debt Traps Threaten Vulnerable Families." October 6, 2016. https://www.americanprogress.org/issues/economy/reports/2016/10/06/145629/how-predatory-debt-traps-threaten-vulnerable-families/.

Chilton, Bruce. *Mary Magdalene: A Biography.* New York: Doubleday, 2005.

"Christ as a mother giving birth to the Church on the cross." Detail from *French Moralized Bible.* 1240. Bodleian Library. Oxford, England.

Cigna. "New Cigna Study Reveals Loneliness at Epidemic Levels in America." May 1, 2018. https://www.cigna.com/newsroom/news-releases/2018/new-cigna-study-reveals-loneliness-at-epidemic-levels-in-america.

Coffin, William Sloane. *Credo.* Louisville: Westminster John Knox, 2004.

D'Anna, John. "'This Anglo man came here to kill Hispanics': After El Paso shooting, will race motivate more violence?" *USA Today,* August 6, 2019. https://www.usatoday.com/story/news/nation/2019/08/06/el-paso-texas-shooting-race-motivate-more-violence/1934948001/.

Davis, Ellen F. *Opening Israel's Scriptures.* New York: Oxford University Press, 2019.

DeBloois, Nanci. "Coins in the New Testament." *BYU Studies Quarterly,* 36 (1996). https://scholarsarchive.byu.edu/cgi/viewcontent.cgi?article=3150&context=byusq.

DeSilver, Drew. "A Record number of women will be serving in the new Congress." *FactTank,* December 18, 2018. https://www.pewresearch.org/fact-tank/2018/12/18/record-number-women-in-congress/.

Devine, Jack with Vernon Loeb. *Good Hunting: An American Spymaster's Story.* New York: Sarah Crichton, 2014.

Donaghue, Erin. "New FBI data shows rise in anti-Semitic hate crimes." *CBS News,* November 13, 2018. https://www.cbsnews.com/news/fbi-hate-crimes-up-new-data-shows-rise-in-anti-semitic-hate-crimes/.

Doyle, John Carroll. "The Coachman." n.d. http://www.johncdoyle.com/repro-detail.php?repoID=44&gcID=3.

Evans, Rachel Held. *A Year of Biblical Womanhood.* Nashville: Thomas Nelson, 2012.

FBI. "2017 Hate Crime Statistics Released: Report Shows More Departments Reporting Hate Crime Statistics." November 13, 2018. https://www.fbi.gov/news/stories/2017-hate-crime-statistics-released-111318.

Felder, Cain Hope, ed. *Stony the Road We Trod: African American Biblical Interpretation.* Minneapolis: Fortress, 1991. Citied in Silliman. "Died: Cain Hope Felder, Scholar Who Lifted Up the Black People in the Bible." *Christianity Today,* October 2, 2019.

Feldman, Lucy. "Most American Women Are Not Optimistic About Electing a Female President: Time Poll. *Time,* November 5, 2018. https://time.com/5443118/american-women-political-engagement/.

Fetti, Domenici. *The Parable of the Lost Drachma.* 1618. oil on panel. Gemäldegaleria Alte Meister. Dresden, Germany.

Fiorenza, Elisabeth Schüssler. *In Memory of Her.* New York: Crossroad, 1987.

Fischer, Kathleen. *Women at the Well.* New York: Paulist, 1988.

Fox, Matthew. *Meister Eckhart: A Mystic-Warrior for Our Times.* California: New World, 2014.

Franciscan Media. "The Truth About Jesus and Women." n.d. https://www.franciscanmedia.org/the-truth-about-jesus-and-women/.

Franco, Aaron and Morgan Radford. "Ex-KKK member denounces hate groups one year after rallying in Charlottesville." *NBC News,* August 9, 2018. https://www.nbcnews.com/news/us-news/ex-kkk-member-denounces-hate-groups-one-year-after-rallying-n899326.

Frank, Anne. *The Diary of a Young Girl: The Definitive Edition.* New York: Anchor, 1991.

Freeman, Lindsey Hardin. *Bible Women: All Their Words and Why They Matter.* Minneapolis: Forward Movement, 2014.

French, David. "The Worst Police Shooting Yet." *National Review,* September 11, 2018. https://www.nationalreview.com/2018/09/amber-guyger-botham-jean-shooting-police-must-face-impartial-justice/.

Geitz, Elizabeth. *Fireweed Evangelism: Christian Hospitality in a Multi-Faith World.* New York: Church Publishing, 2004.

———. *Gender and the Nicene Creed.* Harrisburg, PA: Morehouse, 1995.

———. "Hen Protecting Her Chicks." 2010. Photograph of altar mosaic in Dominus Flevit Church. Mount of Olives, Jerusalem. 8"x10." Geitz Collection.

———. *I Am That Child: Changing Hearts and Changing the World.* New York: Morehouse, 2012.

Gonzales, Richard. "Sessions Cites The Bible To Justify Immigrant Family Separations." *NPR,* June 14, 2018. https://www.npr.org/2018/06/14/620181177/sessions-cites-the-bible-to-justify-immigrant-family-separations.

Green, Emma. "Why the Charlottesville Marchers Were Obsessed With Jews." *The Atlantic,* August 15, 2017. https://www.theatlantic.com/politics/archive/2017/08/nazis-racism-charlottesville/536928/.

Glaser, Chris. "For the Bible Tells Me So: A Study Guide and Advocacy Training Curriculum." *Human Rights Campaign Foundation,* n.d. https://www.hrc.org/resources/for-the-bible-tells-me-so-a-study-guide-and-advocacy-training-curriculum.

Gerig, Bruce L. "The Clobber Passages: Reexamined." *The Epistle.* n.d. http://epistle.us/hbarticles/clobber1.html.

Hagedorn, Ann. *Beyond the River: The Untold Story of the Heroes of the Underground Railroad.* New York: Simon & Schuster, 2002.

Hedges, Chris. *American Fascists: The Christian Right and the War on America.* New York: Free Press, 2007.

Hicks, Brian. "Slavery in Charleston: A chronicle of human bondage in the Holy City." *The Post and Courier,* April 9, 2011. https://www.postandcourier.com/news/special_reports/slavery-in-charleston-a-chronicle-of-human-bondage-in-the/article_54334e04-4834-50b7-990b-f81fa3c2804a.html.

Hoffman, Dr. Joel. *The Bible Doesn't Say That: Biblical Mistranslations, Misconceptions, and Other Misunderstandings.* New York: Thomas Dunne, 2016.

Ifill, Gwen. Interview with Rachel Tiven of Lambda Legal and Mark Potok of the Southern Poverty Law Center. "LGBT Americans target of violent hate crimes more than any other group." Air Date June 13, 2016. https://www.pbs.org/weta/washingtonweek/web-video/lgbt-americans-target-violent-hate-crimes-more-any-other-group.

Intergovernmental Science-Policy Platform on Biodiversity and Ecoservices Report. "Nature's Dangerous Decline 'Unprecedented'; Species Extinction Rates 'Accelerating.'" n.d. https://www.ipbest/news/Media-Release-Global-Assessment.

Jackson, Jesse. "Slave owners and Nazis quote Romans 13 to justify immorality too." *Chicago Sun-Times,* June 18, 2018. https://chicago.suntimes.com/2018/6/18/18405840/slave-owners-and-nazis-quote-romans-13-to-justify-immorality-too.

Jacobi, Tonja and Dylan Schweers. "Female Supreme Court Justices are Interrupted More by Male Justices and Advocates." *Harvard Business Review,* April 11, 2017. https://store.hbr.org/product/female-supreme-court-justices-are-interrupted-more-by-male-justices-and-advocates/h03lr6?sku=H03LR6-PDF-ENG.

Keneally, Meeghan and Bill Hutchinson. "Victims of Dayton and El Paso shootings remembered: 'I'm just speechless.'" *ABC News,* August 7, 2019. https://abcnews.go.com/US/victims-dayton-shooting-remembered-im-speechless/story?id=64780681.

Lechner, Tamara. "6 Reasons Why Laughter is the Best Medicine." *The Chopra Center,* 2016. https://chopra.com/articles/6-reasons-why-laughter-is-the-best-medicine.

Levine, Amy-Jill. *The Misunderstood Jew: The Church and the Scandal of the Jewish Jesus.* New York: Harper One, 2006.

Levine, Suzanne Braun. *You Gotta Have Girlfriends: A Post-Fifty Posse Is Good for Your Health.* New York: Open Road, 2013.

Lewis, Jone Johnson. "Phyllis Schlafly Anti-Feminist Quotes." *ThoughtCo,* n.d. https://www.thoughtco.com/phyllis-schlafly-anti-feminist-quotes-4084041.

Lopez, German. "There are Huge Racial Disparities in How U.S. Police Use Force." *Vox,* November 14, 2018. https://www.vox.com/identities/2016/8/13/17938186/police-shootings-killings-racism-racial-disparities.

MacKinnon, Catherine A. "#MeToo has Done What the Law Could Not." *The New York Times,* February 4, 2018. https://www.nytimes.com/2018/02/04/opinion/metoo-law-legal-system.html.

Mandisa. "That's What Scars Are For." *Overcomer,* August 29, 2013, Sparrow Records. https://www.youtube.com/watch?v=7Gvt__r9EU0.

Mark, Michelle. "Trump just referred to one of his most infamous campaign comments: calling Mexicans 'rapists.'" *Business Insider,* April 5, 2018. https://www.businessinsider.com/trump-mexicans-rapists-remark-reference-2018.

Martin, Clarice J. "Black Theodicy and Black Women's Spiritual Autobiography." In *A Troubling in my Soul: Womanist Perspectives on Evil and Suffering,* edited by Emilie M. Townes, loc. 300–916. Maryknoll, NY: Orbis, 1993.

McAllister, Edward. "Cameroon army helicopters shot separatist protestors: witnesses," October 6, 2017. https://www.reuters.com/article/us-cameroon-protests/cameroon-army-helicopters-shot-separatist-protesters-witnesses-idUSKBN1CB2BP.

Mejia, Zameena. "Just 24 female CEOs lead the companies on the Fortune 500—fewer than last year." *CNBC,* May 21, 2018. https://www.cnbc.com/2018/05/21/2018s-fortune-500-companies-have-just-24-female-ceos.html.

Merritt, Jonathan. "Rachel Held Evans: Christian author was prophet with a pen." *USA Today,* May 7, 2019. https://www.usatoday.com/story/opinion/2019/05/07/rachel-held-evans-christian-author-modern-prophet-future-faith-column/1120983001/.

Misra, Tanvi. "The Cities Refugees Saved." *CityLab,* January 31, 2019. https://www.citylab.com/equity/2019/01/refugee-admissions-resettlement-trump-immigration/580318/.

Montanaro, Domenico. "Americans Largely Support Gun Restrictions To 'Do Something' About Gun Violence." *NPR,* August 10, 2019. https://www.npr.

org/2019/08/10/749792493/americans-largely-support-gun-restrictions-to-do-something-about-gun-violence.

Morford, Mark. "The Sad, Quotable Jerry Falwell." *SF Gate*, May 18, 2007. https://www.sfgate.com/entertainment/morford/article/The-Sad-Quotable-Jerry-Falwell-It-s-bad-form-3302297.php.

Museum of the Bible. "The Slave Bible: Let the Story Be Told." n.d. https://www.museumofthebible.org/exhibits/slave-bible.

National Geographic. "Five Ways Climate Change Will Affect You." n.d. https://www.nationalgeographic.com/climate-change/how-to-live-with-it/index.html.

Nelson, Lee. "How Nurses Cope with Mass Shootings and Attacks." *Nurse.org*, August 16, 2016. https://nurse.org/articles/Nurses-Dealing-With-Long-Term-Mass-Shootings/.

The New York Times Editorial Board. "The Real Meaning of 'Send Her Back!'" July 18, 2019. https://www.nytimes.com/2019/07/18/opinion/trump-rally-send-her-back.html?auth=login-email&login=email.

Nichols, John. "Trump Pick Pence Is a Right-Wing Political Careerist Who Desperately Wants Out of Indiana." *The Nation*, July 14, 2016. https://www.thenation.com/article/likely-trump-pick-pence-is-a-right-wing-political-careerist-who-desperately-wants-out-of-indiana/.

O'Donohue, John. *Anam Cara: A Book of Celtic Wisdom*. New York: Harper Collins, 1998.

Orwell, George. *1984*. Boston: Houghton Mifflin Harcourt, 1949.

PBS. "Interracial Relationships that Changed History." n.d. https://www.pbs.org/black-culture/explore/interracial-marriage-relationships/.

Pilkington, Ed. "Tyler Clementi, student outed as gay on the internet, jumps to his death." *The Guardian*, September 30, 2010. https://www.theguardian.com/world/2010/sep/30/tyler-clementi-gay-student-suicide.

Pope Paul VI. "Marialis Cultus, Apostolic Exhortation." February 2, 1974. http://w2.vatican.va/content/paul-vi/en/apost_exhortations/documents/hf_p-vi_exh_19740202_marialis-cultus.html.

Pritchard, John. *Something More: Encountering the Beyond in the Everyday*. Great Britain: SPCK, 2016.

Quint, Josef, ed. *Meister Eckhart: Die deutschen Werke, vol. III*. Stuttgart, Germany: W. Kohlhammer Verlag, 1958–1976.

Rankin, Rev. John. Published Open Letter, 1841.

Rohr, Richard with Mike Morrell. *The Divine Dance: The Trinity and Your Transformation*. England: SPCK, 2016.

Rosenberg, Yair. "'Jews will not replace us': Why white supremacists go after Jews." *The Washington Post*, August 14, 2017. https://www.washingtonpost.com/news/acts-of-faith/wp/2017/08/14/jews-will-not-replace-us-why-white-supremacists-go-after-jews/.

"The Sandwich Generation." *Senior Living*, n.d. https://www.seniorliving.org/caregiving/sandwich-generation/.

Sacks, Jonathan. *The Dignity of Difference: How to Avoid the Clash of Civilizations.* London: Continuum, 2002.

Sayers, Dorothy L. *Are Women Human? Penetrating, Sensible, and Witty Essays on the Role of Women in Society.* Grand Rapids, MI: Eerdmans, 1971.

Schenk, Christine. "There would have been a midwife at the stable." *National Catholic Reporter,* December 29, 2017. https://www.ncronline.org/news/opinion/simply-spirit/there-would-have-been-midwife-stable.

Schleck, Suzanne. "Mary Magdalene Announcing the Resurrection to the Disciples." 2002, egg tempera and gold leaf on gessoed board, 11"x14." Pennsylvania, Geitz Collection. Original in the Albani Psalter, ca. 1123. Herzog August Biliothek, Wolfenbüttel.

Sheth, Sonam, et al. "7 charts that show the glaring gap between men and women's salaries in the US." *Business Insider,* April 2, 2019. https://www.businessinsider.com/gender-wage-pay-gap-charts-2017-3.

Silliman, Daniel. "Died: Cain Hope Felder, Scholar Who Lifted Up the Black People in the Bible." *Christianity Today,* October 2, 2019. https://www.christianitytoday.com/news/2019/october/died-cain-hope-felder-bible-scholar-african-american.html.

Silverstein, Jason. "There have been more mass shootings than days this year." *CBS News,* August 5, 2019. https://www.cbsnews.com/news/mass-shootings-2019-more-mass-shootings-than-days-so-far-this-year/.

Spak, Kevin. "Limbaugh Takes Racial Swipe at Obama, Oprah." *Newser,* July 8, 2010. https://www.newser.com/story/94972/limbaugh-takes-racial-swipe-at-obama-oprah.html.

Stiepleman, Daniel. *On the Basis of Sex.* Film. Directed by Mimi Leder. California: Focus Features, 2018.

Thunberg, Greta. "Our House is On Fire." *#FridaysForFuture,* January 22, 2019. https://www.fridaysforfuture.org/greta-speeches#greta_speech_jan22_2019.

Tissot, James J. *The Lost Drachma.* 1886–1894, opaque watercolor over graphite on gray wove paper, Brooklyn Museum, Brooklyn, New York.

Tobin, Jacqueline L. and Raymond G. Dobard. *Hidden in Plain View: A Secret Story of Quilts and the Underground Railroad.* New York: Anchor Books, 1999.

Trotter, Elizabeth. "Why the Apostle Paul Compared Himself to a Nursing Mother." *For Every Mom,* September 12, 2017. https://foreverymom.com/faith/apsotle-paul-nursing-mother-elizabeth-trotter/.

Tuckman, Jo. "'We've been taken hostage': African migrants stranded in Mexico after Trump's crackdown." *The Guardian,* September 30, 2019. https://www.theguardian.com/us-news/2019/sep/30/weve-been-taken-hostage-african-migrants-stranded-in-mexico-after-trumps-crackdown.

Tutu, Desmond. "#ShareTheJoy message from Archbishop Desmond Tutu." Desmond Tutu Facebook page. n.d. https://www.facebook.com/watch/?v=887134008097266.

UN Women. "Facts and Figures: Young Women's Leadership." n.d. https://www.unwomen.org/en/what-we-do/youth/facts-and-figures.

UNESCO. "Education for All Global Monitoring Report." October 2013. https://en.unesco.org/gem-report/sites/gem-report/files/girls-factsheet-en.pdf.

Vines, Matthew. *God and the Gay Christian: The Biblical Case in Support of Same-Sex Relationships*. New York: Convergent, 2014.

Vox.com. "After Sandy Hook We Said Never Again." Updated daily. https://www.vox.com/a/mass-shootings-america-sandy-hook-gun-violence.

Weiner, Tim. *Legacy of Ashes: The History of the CIA*. New York: Anchor, 2008.

Williams, Delores S. *Sisters in the Wilderness: The Challenge of Womanist God-Talk*. New York: Orbis, 1993.

Wink, Walter. *Homosexuality and Christin Faith: Questions of Conscience for the Churches*. Minneapolis: Augsburg Fortress, 1999.

Worley, Will. "Thousands of Palestinian and Israeli women join to march through desert together for peace." *The Independent*, October 8, 2017. https://www.independent.co.uk/news/world/middle-east/palestinian-israeli-women-peace-march-desert-a7989216.html.

Wortman, Julie A. "The Gospel vs. Scripture? Biblical Theology and the Debate about Rites of Blessing: An Interview with Walter Brueggemann." *The Other Journal*, October 10, 2004. https://theotherjournal.com/2004/10/10/the-gospel-vs-scripture-biblical-theology-and-the-debate-about-rites-of-blessing-an-interview-with-walter-brueggemann/.

Would Jesus Discriminate? "David Loved Jonathan More Than Women." n.d. http://www.wouldjesusdiscriminate.org/biblical_evidence/david_jonathan.html. See also Minor, Jeff and John Tyler Connoley. *The Children Are Free: Reexamining the Biblical Evidence on Same-Sex Relationships*. Indianapolis: LifeJourney Press, 2002.

Yerman, Marcia G. "Amy Ferris Takes on Depression in 'Shades of Blue.'" *Huffington Post*, December 6, 2017. https://www.huffpost.com/entry/amy-ferris-takes-on-depre_b_9435438.

Young, William Paul. *The Shack*. Newbury Park, CA: Windblown Media, 2007.

Young, Yvette, et al., "Let's Talk About Race and Human Trafficking." *Love146*, June 4, 2019. https://love146.org/lets-talk-about-race-and-human-trafficking/.

Yousafzai, Malala with Christina Lamb. *I Am Malala: The Girl Who Stood Up for Education and Was Shot By the Taliban*. New York: Little Brown, 2013.

Zauzmer, Julie. "What draws women to a religion that says men should be in charge?" *The Washington Post*, September 21, 2018. https://www.washingtonpost.com/religion/2018/09/21/what-draws-women-religion-that-says-men-should-be-charge/.

Zezima, Katie and Samantha Henry. "N.J. works to curb sex trafficking at Super Bowl." *USA Today*, January 6, 2014. https://www.usatoday.com/story/news/nation/2014/01/06/nj-sex-trafficking-super-bowl/4338361/.

Zremski, Jerry. "Study: Women presidential candidates endure tougher coverage." *The Buffalo News*, April 14, 2019. https://buffalonews.com/2019/04/14/study-women-presidential-candidates-endure-tougher-coverage/.

Scripture Index

**HEBREW BIBLE/
OLD TESTAMENT**

Genesis

1:27, 31	30–31
1:28	32–33
2:18, 22	34
2:22–23	35–36
3:16	37–38
5:1–2	39–40
9:6	46
17:4–6	78–79
18:1–15	98
19:1–11	66–67
21:16–17	47–48

Exodus

1:15–17	106–07
2:7	108
6:6	49–50
15:20	109
19:3–4	6
20:13	102–03
21:7	68
23:9	88–89
35:2	68

Leviticus

20:13	68-69

Numbers

12:1, 5, 9	51–52
27:1-7	110

Deuteronomy

10:17–18	90–91
23:15	55–56
32:18	7

Joshua

2:4–5	111

Judges

4:4–5	112–13
13:6, 9	144–45

Ruth

1:16	148

1 Samuel

18:1–4	73–74
20:30	73
25:32–35	114

2 Samuel

1:26	73–74

1 Kings

10:1–2	115

2 Kings

22:14	116–17

Esther

4:15–16	119

Job

9:1, 10:10–12	8–9
38:1, 8	10

Psalms

2	15
13:1	94–95
22:9–10	11–12
30:11–12	146–47
37	15
42:1	149–50
46:10	151
82:4	57–58
104:1, 10–12	152–53
118:23	92–93
139:13	13–14

Song of Solomon

7:10–13, 8:1–3	118

Isaiah

42:5, 14	2
43:1	70
43:2–3	71–72
45:19, 46:3–4	4
46:3–4, 9	5
66:12–14	3

Jeremiah

30:5–6	15–16
38:7–13	53–54

Hosea

13:4, 8	17

Amos

5:24–26	59–60

Micah

6:1, 4	109

NEW TESTAMENT

Matthew

10:11–15	66
22:39	51
25:35–36	96–97
27:19	130
27:45, 50	23

28:18, 20	154
35:55–56	131–32

Mark

9:2–5	80–81
10:5–6	41
14:6, 9	122

Luke

1:39, 56	120–121
2:36–38	123
4:38–39	124
8:1–2	125–26
10:8–12	66
10:39–42	127
13:34	18–19
15:8–9	20–21
24:1–4	133
24:13–27	98
24:29	98

John

4:7–9, 27–28, 39	128
8:32	165–66
10:10	155
10:20	155
11:21–27	129
14:6	82
16:16, 20–22	22
18:38	167
20:11, 17-18	134–35

Acts

2:17	42
9:1–6	83–84
16:14–15	136

Romans

1:1, 7, 16:1	137–138
1:1, 7, 16:7	139
1:1, 7, 8:22–23	61
12:2	156
13:1–2	100–101
16:3–5	140

1 Corinthians

13:12	166
14:34–35	43

2 Corinthians

4:8–9   157–58

Galatians

3:28   85–86

4:1, 19   26–27

Ephesians

4:25   159

Philippians

4:1–3   141–42

4:8   160

1 Thessalonians

1:1, 2:7–8   28

5:16   161–62

1 Timothy

2:12   43

2 Timothy

2:2–4   163–64

Hebrews

2:14, 17   25

13:2   98–99

James

4:12   62–63

Made in the USA
Columbia, SC
16 January 2020

86864727R00113